BY YUNG PUEBLO

How to Love Better

Lighter

THE INWARD TRILOGY

Inward

Clarity & Connection

The Way Forward

HOW TO LOVE BETTER

How to Love Better

the path to deeper connection through growth, kindness, and compassion

Yung Pueblo

HARMONY
NEW YORK

Published in the United States by Harmony Books,
an imprint of Random House, a division of
Penguin Random House LLC, New York.

Harmony Books is a registered trademark, and the Circle colophon is a trademark of Penguin Random House LLC.

Yung Pueblo® is a registered trademark.

LIBRARY OF CONGRESS CATALOGING-IN-PUBLICATION DATA
Names: Yung Pueblo (Writer), author.
Title: How to love better / by Yung Pueblo.
Description: First edition. | New York, NY: Harmony, [2025] |
Identifiers: LCCN 2024040970 (print) |
LCCN 2024040971 (ebook) | ISBN 9780593582275 (hardcover) |
ISBN 9780593582282 (ebook)
Subjects: LCSH: Love. | Interpersonal relations. |
Interpersonal conflict.
Classification: LCC BF575.L8 Y86 2025 (print) |
LCC BF575.L8 (ebook) |
DDC 152.4/1—dc23/eng/20241022
LC record available at https://lccn.loc.gov/2024040970
LC ebook record available at https://lccn.loc.gov/2024040971

Printed in the United States of America on acid-free paper

HarmonyBooks.com | RandomHouseBooks.com

2 4 6 8 9 7 5 3 1

First Edition

Book design based on a design by Andrea Lau
Ornament by ku4erashka/Adobe Stock

For Sara,

my wife and comrade in wisdom

contents

The three biggest green flags are
growth, kindness, and compassion.

If they are consistently kind,
if they care about growing,
and if they can see beyond
their own perspective,
then this is someone worth
your time and energy.

Deep love is not easy because it contains so much.

It is full of disagreements, howling laughter,
hard conversations, genuine care, plenty of tears,
undeniable joy, and the feeling of being truly seen.

You don't get the good without the tough stuff
that helps you both grow.

introduction

Our Story

We met quite young, both of us still finding our footing in college, but as soon as we were in each other's gravity, Sara and I felt an undeniable pull that kept bringing us even closer together. We became friends first, talking, connecting, enjoying the other's company late into the night, sharing stories and paying attention to each other as if it were the first time that someone was truly listening. We both felt a new sense of joy that was unlocked when we were together. We felt removed from everyone else, even removed from time, existing in a space that was just for the two of us. We loved being in our own world, a place where we could share our secrets and think about things together. It was enlivening and, at times, all-consuming. Soon, our feelings for each other grew and friendship alone could no longer encapsulate the depth of our connection. After just two weeks of officially being a couple, we told each other "I love you"—both of us were telling the truth, but neither of us realized yet that love is more than a feeling; it's a practice that needs intention, care, and skill.

As months went by, the gaps in our ability to love started revealing themselves in painful and tense ways. We fought often and we fought bitterly, meeting anger with anger; we both did our best to win each tiny battle. Blame became a common mode of communication. We kept throwing our internal tension, stress, and irritation on each other, wanting to make it the other's fault when we didn't feel good inside. We couldn't take responsibility for our own bad mood and tried relentlessly to drag the other down into the heaviness we felt in our minds. These moments of intensity were quite frequent. We felt so strongly about each other, but we did not know how to care for our own emotions or how to support the other's happiness. Shouldn't the fact that we wanted to create a life together be enough? We both felt like something was wrong, but we couldn't get it right. Why were we always arguing? When would the other realize that they needed to act better?

In our first few years together, we were caught in a state of confusion. It felt like an emotional hurricane that would move at different levels of intensity. We barely made it through that period—we actually broke up a few times and took a few breaks because we didn't know if it was the right thing for us to be together. Each break and breakup was short-lived because we couldn't stand being apart, but the difficulty was that we also didn't know how to be together well. Ultimately, we decided that we wanted to struggle together rather than be apart. Even if disharmony was frequent, we decided to keep facing it and hopefully find a better way. We lived like this for six years, swimming between short-lived calmness and awful storms.

The connection was undeniable, but neither of us knew how to love well. We didn't know where to begin or what to aim for. We didn't know that the balance we were looking for and the peace we so desperately wanted could not come from one of us giving them to the other, but instead they had to come from within each of us. Cultivating peace and compassion within our own minds was the only way to create a bridge between the two of us that would be stable enough to support a more nourishing relationship. The beginning of our relationship was so stormy because we were completely unaware of our individual inner worlds and certainly did not know that what we felt inside was always impacting our perceptions and actions. Neither of us realized that connection alone could not fill the vastness of love and that the undeniable pull we felt toward each other was not enough to create peace between us.

It's a total lie that relationships
are supposed to be easy.

You have to learn how to love each other well
while the relationship shines a mirror
on the ways you each need to grow.

This is a big challenge to accept.

Our only experience of love was chaotic because neither of us understood how our own lack of personal emotional maturity and self-awareness created blocks that stopped us from engaging with each other in a wiser and more compassionate manner.

After years of struggle, the answer quietly came into our lives. A dear friend of ours started meditating and both Sara and I felt an instinctive pull to try meditating too. We were exhausted by our personal and relational tension and wanted to find an answer to the riddle of suffering and angst that was consistently making our days as individuals, and as a couple, heavier. We were tired of the struggle and open to trying something new.

At the time, we didn't realize that we had just flipped the page into a new era of our relationship. Who we were and how we acted gradually evolved as we kept attending silent meditation retreats, and eventually we each began a daily practice. Little bits of peace slowly started entering our lives, tiny beams of light started brightening the tumultuous darkness that we both carried inside of us. Meditating not only helped us be better versions of ourselves, but the self-awareness that we were both cultivating started encouraging us to treat each other more gently. The healing that we were going through on the deepest level was resulting in calmer minds, more presence, and more compassion for ourselves and each other. The blame game that we were locked into was in time revealed to be completely counter-productive. Each argument did not need to end with a clear winner and loser; the light of awareness revealed that what was really missing was sincere listening and understanding.

You know the connection is special
when the person who wants to be
with you also understands that they
need to put energy into learning
how to love you well.

They know that love is not automatic;
instead it comes from deep listening
and doing their best to meet your
preferences in a way that feels genuine.

Meditating changed everything for us. It showed us how to love better, and it did so by helping us both cultivate mental qualities that we were missing, like awareness, nonreactiveness, and compassion. We were aware of these concepts and actions, but they were qualities of the mind that were woefully undeveloped. A lot of the misery that we shared came from our inability to hold space for our own difficult emotions. We both began meditating as a way to gain inner peace; we did not realize that this mental training was also the remedy that our relationship desperately needed. We lacked the awareness to see that our inner pain was intrinsically connected to our outer struggle and causing us to unconsciously react to each other with tension.

Meditating did not immediately fix everything. But the honest truth is that applying meditation to our daily lives over an extended period of time (many years) is what ultimately transformed our relationship for the better. As we each grew in the practice of meditation, as we accepted more responsibility for how we felt, and as we better understood what we genuinely needed from each other to thrive as a couple, peace started slowly entering our relationship.

Our relationship today is not perfect. We still argue and disagree from time to time, but now we have the inner fortitude to hold each other with compassion as we process what we feel. Arguments no longer turn into full-blown hurricanes, instead they become opportunities for both of us to take turns listening so that we can try to see beyond our own perspectives and get to the real root of what is upsetting us. We do not expect our relationship to be endlessly peaceful and joyous, but we do now have the tools to navigate the challenging moments more smoothly and quickly.

The power of meditation is not just in the fact that it helped us with deep personal healing and over time brought us together as a couple in a more harmonious way, but that it also clarifies certain universal truths that can be applied to individuals and relationships.

I've spent the last twelve years meditating seriously. During that time I have meditated over twelve thousand hours. In no way do I consider myself an expert. In fact I benefit much more from seeing myself as a perpetual student, and I look forward to continuing to meditate in the future so that I can keep growing and learning. Even so, this dedication to inner practice has already transformed my life and helped me move confidently into the world of writing. Under the pen name Yung Pueblo, I have focused my writing at the intersection of personal growth and relationships. I take the attention you give my writing as a heartfelt responsibility. Your trust is something that I want to treat genuinely and gently. What I can offer you are the understandings and explorations that have brought peace into my own mind and life and more harmony into the connections that I cherish.

In this book I offer my reflections on love. The main focus of this book will be its exact title, *How to Love Better*. Though I will concentrate on the love between significant others, everything here can be applied to all important relationships in our lives. We all know something about love already because we are human beings. And we are all experts at knowing what different emotions feel like—we move through them on a daily basis, we struggle with them, we enjoy them, and we learn from them. The purpose of this book revolves around the fact that even though we are familiar with our own emotional ranges, we can benefit from improving our understanding of ourselves and how we relate to what we feel. In the act of knowing yourself better, you will be able to love your partner better and allow the vehicle of love to propel your personal growth. Love and growth need to go hand in hand for harmony to be a real possibility in a partnership.

> Relationship, surely, is the mirror in which you
> discover yourself. . . . To be, is to be related;
> to be related is existence.
>
> —*Jiddu Krishnamurti*

Love has the shape
and feel of water.

It is simultaneously
flexible and powerful.

It can adapt and roar;
it can also be silently nourishing.

Instead of looking for
someone who is "perfect,"
look for someone
who is not scared of growing.

The beginnings of relationships
are not always smooth.

Even when the connection is strong
you still have to intentionally learn
how to love each other well.

HOW TO LOVE BETTER

chapter 1

How to Help Love Flow

Love is one of the clearest feelings a human being can experience, yet it is too enigmatic to place a concrete definition on. Like trying to grab water with your hand, the exact limits of love are rightfully elusive, but even so, we can get close to giving words to its depth.

Love is a powerful and liberating feeling—one that radiates throughout your body. Love is a light that can shine brightly from within you even when you are alone, and it is also a light that intensifies between two people when the magnetic feeling between them has proven to be undeniable. Love is an energy that motivates you into action. It helps the mind see clearly and selflessly. Love helps you come in contact with your strength and courage. It helps you say the things you were once afraid to voice. Love can help you say no, and, equally, it can help you full-heartedly say yes. It helps you clarify what is and is not important.

In the pantheon of human emotions, love stands as the most prized experience. It is something we seek actively and passively. We may seek it in the form of self-love as a way to heal and free ourselves or in the form of a healthy and nourishing partnership. In either case, arriving at one of these forms of love provides a great level of rest, solace, and happiness to our being. All of the friendships and close relationships we pour energy and attention into are also included in the foundation of our lives. We are relational beings: We not only depend on others for survival but thrive in relationships with others.

Love is not something small. It is the energy of love that often changes lives and even history. Love has the power to break down walls and open doorways. It also has the power to preserve, create boundaries, and make tough calls. Love is deeply personal and highly situational. The way one person loves themselves can be totally different from how another activates self-love in their life. The way one couple expresses love can be miles away from the next. Even though love can look different for everyone, it always has that warm feeling of safety and freedom when it is brought to life.

The purpose of this book is to deeply explore how love manifests in partnerships and to answer the question, "How can I love better?"

WHERE WE STRUGGLE AND HOW WE RISE

The deep truth is that most human beings do not arrive into a relationship unscathed from the ups and downs of life. From childhood to adulthood, life leaves its mark on your mind many times over, and these marks morph into patterns that are often coping mechanisms or defensive tactics you picked up while you were in survival mode. The hurt you have accumulated ultimately shapes the way you perceive reality and can even form walls that have to be broken down so you can fully love yourself and others.

To be able to love your partner well, a deep reckoning needs to happen where you realize that how you love and heal yourself has a direct connection to how you show up in your relationship. The relationship between you and yourself has a clear impact on the relationship between you and your partner. If you want to love your partner better, then you need to develop a two-pronged approach:

1. Improving your relationship with yourself by letting go of the heaviness that your mind carries

2. Working to outwardly shift your behaviors so they can be more conducive to a harmonious relationship

Love is not easy, and it is honestly a lot of work. Love is a powerful mirror where you cannot help but see yourself clearly; it will show you how you have grown, and it will show you in which direction you need to grow next. Being in a relationship is not about living in a constant stream of pleasure. Even the healthiest relationships will be full of ups and downs and unforeseen challenges. A relationship should certainly provide comfort, joy, and a sense of safety, but it should also become fuel for your evolution. Once you embrace your growth, the new harmony that starts flowing within you will help support the harmony in your relationship.

One of the biggest internal things to overcome so that love can flow better between two people is attachment. The human mind has a powerful drive to crave for things to exist in a manner that is to our liking, but sometimes this drive will turn an unproblematic desire into a strong attachment that has gathered so much mental tension that we feel upset when things diverge from what we initially imagined. The drive to set things up the way we like them can become controlling if it remains unchecked. Love is meant to support the feeling of freedom when in the presence of your partner, but attachment can squander that feeling when you demand things happen the way you want them to.

The key to harmony in a relationship is finding a balance between making sure that your genuine needs are met, and establishing clear and voluntary commitments that help support each other's happiness. You both know that you cannot directly make the other happy because happiness is something that emerges from your personal mindset, but together you can create the conditions and environment where it is easier to feel joy and fulfillment in each other's presence. A partnership can bring so much delight into your life, but only you can clarify your perspective so you can let joy in and experience happiness more often.

Establishing these commitments helps reduce attachment and confusion. Commitments are the application of honest and open communication so you both learn how to love each other well by voicing your needs. When you hear each other's needs, you can then check in with yourselves and see what feels good to commit to. This lets you both show up in your relationship in a way that feels driven by your desire to love your partner well as opposed to feeling pressured by your partner to behave in a certain way.

Forcing, controlling, possessiveness, manipulation—these are all variations of attachment. They are unmistakable blocks that stop love from flowing and they create pressure on a relationship in a way that eventually breaks the connection. Love is meant to uplift, a partnership is meant to nourish—attachment does the opposite. It is a self-centered approach to a relationship that can end something great before it even really begins.

If you think a relationship
is meant to be an escape
or that it should only be blissful,
then you're missing the point.

Love is soft and nourishing,
but it is also hard and revealing.
It will show you the sides of
yourself that you need to work on.

One of the most crucial elements of love is selflessness. This means knowing yourself well enough that you can see beyond your own ego, cravings, and attachments and are able to intentionally arrive into your relationship as someone who wants to make your partner's happiness as much of a priority as your own. Developing selflessness helps you nourish a balance between giving and receiving, two qualities that are important for both partners to work on. Both need to be able to give so the other feels taken care of, and both need to be able to receive so that the effort of their partner is not wasted. Selflessness is what allows patience, listening, and understanding to really thrive.

Three Overarching Qualities That Can Help You Love Better

1. **Kindness.** Kindness is vastly underrated and is key in demonstrating to your partner that you care about them. Treating your partner as your friend and loved one, even when you two are going through a tough moment, is a clear application of kindness. When an argument is happening, you may have to remind yourself that your partner is not your enemy, it is not you versus them, it is actually the two of you versus your different understandings or miscommunication.

   Holding kindness as the medium through which you

interact with each other is a direct sign of your love. Kindness is a form of gentleness that helps soften your actions. Since your partner is your closest comrade in life, the one you spend the most time with, it makes sense to intentionally treat them with kindness.

It is easy to get stuck in a mode where we often give our partners the hardest parts of ourselves. They see us when we are most angry or upset, and really this is because we feel so comfortable around them that we can finally put our guard down and be the realest version of ourselves. Our partners see us when we are dejected and exhausted, they see the toughest parts of our character, and this is actually a beautiful thing, that we can be vulnerable with them, but it needs to be balanced so they can enjoy the best parts of us too.

In the same way that we can show our partner the rawest parts of our emotions, we should be intentional about treating them with kindness so that the relationship isn't overwhelmed with down moments.

2. **Growth.** One of the best ways to love your partner better is by embracing growth and development as a lifelong journey. When you have the humility to realize that there is so much for you to learn and that you can benefit greatly from stepping outside of your comfort zone, your personal evolution will come more naturally.

This ability to welcome growth into your life is one of the greatest gifts you can give yourself and your partner. No one enters a relationship fully healed, completely wise, or perfect in their ability to love. Real love requires learning, adapting, letting go, and reaching new levels of peace and understanding.

Especially when you are looking for a serious relationship, this quality is the greenest of green flags. No one is perfect and everyone makes mistakes, but finding someone who takes responsibility and is open to correcting their mistakes and expanding beyond their old limits shows they are more likely to have the inner strength and skills to get through the hard moments of a relationship.

When both partners embrace growth, the real magic of a relationship flourishes. Without this quality, moments of difficulty in the relationship become roadblocks that you can't get around. With this quality you can see the difficulty, examine why it is there, understand your separate roles in this challenge, and cultivate new qualities that can help you persevere and reach a new level.

Love is not static; it flows. Love loves change. When you can each accept that you are ever-changing beings, it makes it easier to adapt when your preferences and understandings evolve as you spend time together. Who you are when you first start your relationship is not who you will be as your relationship moves forward in the river of time. Change is bound to happen, and if you let it, it can make your love even stronger.

This makes sense when you realize that your relationship will go through different chapters and how you love each other in one chapter may shift in another. Your commitment to growth will smooth the transition from one way of loving each other into another. Especially if you are together for years or decades, the way you show love to each other will need to adapt to meet your evolving preferences. Human beings are innately change oriented; whether the changes are small or large, they are always happening.

A growth-oriented mindset helps you have the flexibility to see love as a long-term project and yourself as an eternal student.

3. **Compassion.** This is probably the biggest and most important differentiator between relationships that have harmony and those that do not. An essential way to show compassion is to intentionally practice putting yourself in your partner's shoes. Try to selflessly see the world and situations through their lens. It takes a lot of humility and strength to set aside your own perspective for a moment and place yourself in your partner's, especially if

you two are going through a tough moment or when you are in the middle of an argument.

Compassion is such a necessary skill because it helps you uncover your own blocks. When you step outside of your own perspective, you can literally see more. It is easier to just stick with your own view, but love challenges you to grow by taking your partner's emotions seriously. If you can only see things your way, then you will struggle greatly in supporting your partner's happiness.

Compassion not only helps you see your partner better, but it also helps you learn their mind and heart. Compassion is the energy you use to learn more about your partner's emotional history; it helps you study your partner so you can become familiar with their triggers and their preferences. Without compassion, your partner would remain a mystery to you. Communication is always part of the solution, but what isn't talked about enough is how important it is to see your partner's perspective as something that is as important as your own.

Compassion is related to kindness because they both contain the element of gentleness, but compassion takes it further by combining gentleness with an expanded perspective and action. You are not only trying to understand your partner better, but you are also trying to act on what you are learning about them.

Granted, in all three qualities, it works only if both people are actively trying to cultivate them. One-sided relationships, where one person is doing all the emotional heavy lifting, are often unsustainable. This doesn't mean that you both have to behave the same way or have the same preferences. You will certainly have different strong points in your relationship, but there should be a sense of balance and a feeling that you are both receiving amply. It takes two to feed a relationship so that it can really succeed.

For many people, healthy relationships where self-awareness is encouraged, where communication is clear and open, where growth is welcome, are a new phenomenon. It feels like we are living in a time when millions of people in the world are learning how to love themselves and one another better. We are trying to break away from the old idea of love, that our relationships should always be perfect and make our lives easier, into a more nuanced and realistic view of love. The type of love where we are not afraid of tough moments and challenges, because we know overcoming them will actually elevate the love that is shared between two people.

So much of the media and fairy tales around love hide the reality that love takes a lot of intentional work to make it vibrant. Two people can feel love for each other, but more of us are understanding that it takes time to really learn how to care for each other. We are also learning how important it is to know ourselves more deeply so our past doesn't stop us from loving our partner fully. Love doesn't immediately create a home; it has to be carefully and intentionally constructed by two patient people who feel safe to be their most real selves with each other. Love is a journey.

Relationships that are nourishing
don't just happen without any work.

You have to design a culture that takes
into account your separate emotional
histories, your needs, your communication
styles, your goals, and more.

Being open about the way you
want to be loved sets your
partner up for success.

HOW TO LOVE BETTER

Everyone enters relationships with a multitude of imperfections. Depending on the person and their emotional history, there can be a wide range of internal matters that are unresolved: hurt from the past, negative behavior patterns, unrealistic expectations, fears—there are so many things that can form blockages in the flow of love and make it more difficult for us to connect deeply.

Since ego is so predominant in daily life, it will naturally and consistently impede the selflessness, kindness, and patience needed to support the harmony of a relationship. Attachment and the craving to control, which are intertwined with ego, also stand as roadblocks that each individual has to gradually undo if they want to enjoy a peaceful and fulfilling connection.

In many ways, a relationship is an opportunity to learn how to love better. When we accept this framework, it becomes easier to use the lessons that arise to transform our behavior, for our own benefit and for the benefit of our partner. Even though love comes with its challenges, the depth of the connection creates an immediate incentive to try to work on ourselves so that we can treat our partners better and give the relationship a better chance to thrive.

Nine Strategies That Can Help You Love Better

1. **When both of you take your healing seriously, the relationship wins.** You both carry baggage from the past. Even if you haven't experienced deep trauma, there are still tendencies and patterns that have developed over time because the way you react accumulates in the mind. Through learning how to let go, you can stop past unproductive patterns from taking over. Developing your self-love is the necessary foundation that will support all relationships in your life. It is not selfish to learn what you need to do to take care of yourself and consistently put it into action so you can show up as the best version of yourself. Remember, you and your partner may need different healing tools, but make sure that you are using something that is genuinely making you more self-aware and mentally lighter. Meditation and therapy have helped millions of people. Find what works for you.

2. **Enter the relationship knowing that you will have to grow to make it work.** Embracing your imperfections is a superpower that opens the door to personal evolution. Partnerships can be a potent catalyst for growth when you accept the challenge. As soon as the connection begins, start reflecting on your major past patterns and think about what you can do differently this time to

create a thriving environment between you and your partner.

3. **Everything is not always their fault.** Tension can easily twist your reasoning and make you place all the blame on your partner whenever conflict arises. Sometimes they are going to make mistakes and will apologize to you, but there will also be times when you make mistakes and need to apologize. Being able to recognize and own the fact that you started a fight is a big sign of inner strength. When both people can check themselves and try to find the real root of their tension, it helps decrease the intensity of an argument.

4. **In the midst of an argument, remember that this is the person you love, and they are not your enemy.** Your past can cloud your perception and make you become hyper defensive. Learn how to pull yourself out of survival mode. Being able to ground yourself can help you let go of anger and move from having an argument to simply hearing each other's side of the story so you can find a healthy middle ground. Reframe your idea of an argument from a battle to an opportunity that helps you understand each other better.

5. **If you both focus on giving, you will each receive more.** This one only works if both people are truly com-

mitted to taking care of their partner in multiple ways. Only with open hands can you give and receive; love is an active expression of this sentiment. The way you give to each other may not always look the same because each individual has different strengths and preferences.

6. **Move with honesty and gentleness.** The truth, even when it is hard to give or receive, will ultimately bring you closer together. Lies and withheld truths create blockages in your connection. Truth should be delivered in a compassionate and skillful manner. Speaking to each other with gentleness, even when you are in a tense moment, will help keep you both levelheaded.

7. **Ask each other "How can I love you better?" and act on it.** It is helpful to get new information from your partner directly because, just like you, they are an ever-changing being. Their preferences will slowly shift over time and knowing them can help you better offer support as they move through their ups and downs. Relationships go through seasons, so it's good to check in regularly.

8. **View each other as best friends; this will help with deep and enjoyable communication.** Try not to fall into the stagnancy of speaking only about mundane topics, like your jobs and taking care of errands—these are

obviously important but there is so much more to explore together. Keep learning about each other by having discussions about your beliefs, examining how your past has impacted your present, what's going on in the world, how you each think the universe works, your future goals, the directions you'd like to grow in, and whatever else is enriching and enlivening to talk about.

9. **Do not try to control each other.** Love will always be about freedom. Healthy relationships will keep the feeling of freedom vibrant. Of course, you will design your life together and voluntarily commit to each other in ways that feel good to both of you, but neither partner should ever feel coerced or like they don't have a say in how they live their life. Ultimately, you are two individuals who are creating a home together, but you both still have your own lives to tend to. You are two streams that have chosen to flow together side by side. Loving each other better is about supporting each other's happiness.

Love is not just comfort—it is also growth. Refusing to understand this truth is what breaks a lot of relationships. We often think of love in terms of what we want from it, but not in terms of the ways we need to grow to nurture it. Relationships are innately revealing, especially when the connection is deep and undeniable. The tricky thing is that you can feel love toward a person without knowing how to practice love in a way that feels mutually fulfilling and uplifting. The other challenge is that the practice of love is two people creating a world for themselves that not only feels generative and nourishing, but also is designed to meet the unique needs, wants, and commitments that are personal to their relationship. No matter how you evoke the practice of love, it is necessary to understand that love will show you where you need to grow. It will help you see the parts of you that need more light and it will give you an opportunity to cultivate habits and behavior styles that produce harmony and understanding. If you want to love well in the present, you will have to work on letting go of the past.

Reflection Questions

- What does your ideal relationship look like? What does it feel like?
- Are you successful at seeing other people's perspectives?
- What have you learned about yourself that has helped you show up better in your relationship?
- What do you need to feel loved?
- Do you and your partner ask each other "How can I love you better?" If not, can you challenge yourself to do this?

chapter 2

The Relationship Between You and Yourself

Before you can truly examine where you stand in your ability to love well, you must first take a deep and honest look at yourself and consider how expansively love flows within your own being. Not only within your own mind and heart, but how does it manifest in your habits and behaviors?

Are you a friend to your own emotions? Can you stand and face your inner landscape as you are going through tumultuous experiences? Are you familiar with your own emotional history? Do you have a sense of how your past has molded your character and your present-day behaviors?

The last big question is: Are you loving yourself well? The answer to this will give you a good sense of your capacity to love another being. Loving yourself well means not just caring for your body, mind, and heart but also having an identity that embraces change. One where you encourage yourself to let go of old aspects of yourself that no longer support your flourishing and bring in new qualities that will help you show up for yourself and others more profoundly. Having a mindset that embraces your own growth is what helps you heal and unbind the negative patterns that are driven by your difficult past experiences. Evolution is necessary.

ON SELF-AWARENESS

Humility is a necessary characteristic that can help you have a peaceful mind and propel you into deep growth. Being humble comes from grounding yourself in the fact that there is always more to learn and it does not help to be egocentric or to think that you are better than others. True humility actually throws away comparison; it is a state of mind that does not look at life as a competition, and you can appreciate where you are and where others are without judgment. Being humble does not mean you are not confident in your skills; you can silently know your strengths without bragging about them in your mind or to others. Being humble simply means you are open, that your sense of self is calm and flexible, that you allow curiosity to lead as opposed to defensiveness and fear. Humility and wisdom go hand in hand, because the depths of liberational wisdom cannot be accessed with a thick ego. The energy of a humble person is quite disarming; it is easy to relax around them and to connect with them because you do not fear being ridiculed.

There is an undeniable connection between the relationship you have with yourself and the relationship you have with another. If you cannot see yourself, then you will certainly struggle to see another well. This is why the cultivation of self-awareness is critical not only for those seeking a fulfilling life, but also for anyone who understands the value of appreciating the perspective of another.

Self-awareness helps you see that within you there is a vast universe, one filled with a variety of emotions, viewpoints, patterns, and so much more. It helps you embrace the complexity that gives you your identity. When you can appreciate your own depth and the range of your own emotions, it starts to dawn on you that you are not the only one who feels so much. You start deeply appreciating that the same way you struggle, others struggle too. Self-awareness opens the door to compassion.

You cannot see the depth of your imperfections, the mistakes you have made in the past and moments in your life where you could have made better choices, without the power of self-awareness. Self-awareness is not meant to be a quality that produces the feeling of regret, instead it is meant to encourage the development of objective observation so that you can understand who you are and what you have gone through.

Self-awareness helps you take an honest survey so that you can move forward with all the information that you need to adjust your actions. You need to be able to see what is there before you can learn from it and grow. Self-awareness helps you see that perfection is not possible, but progress is. It helps you take responsibility for your own actions and gives you insight into other people. When you can come to terms with the ups and downs of your own life, patience and compassion start blooming for yourself and other people.

My actions are my only true belongings.
I cannot escape the consequences of my actions.
My actions are the ground on which I stand.
—Thich Nhat Hanh's translation of the Anguttara Nikaya 5.57

Self-awareness also helps you pierce through a lot of the mental conditioning that you never asked for, but that we all accumulate through life anyway. Through self-awareness you discover your genuine preferences and aspirations, not the things society wants you to strive for, but what authentically feels nourishing for you to spend your energy on. I didn't know I wanted to be a writer until I started meditating. I remember in my third silent ten-day meditation course I felt my intuition strongly encouraging me to write. It took me a long time to listen to that guidance and gather the courage to take it seriously.

Self-awareness essentially becomes a training ground for the development of qualities that will impact the relationship you have with yourself and with other people. As your self-awareness grows, you become less demanding and more accepting. Instead of craving perfection, you start working with the fact that imperfection is unavoidable.

Some people develop self-awareness through journaling, others through meditation, and some through the straightforward practice of not running away from their emotions when they feel turbulent. Self-awareness grows with all reflection and when the knowledge you are accruing about yourself starts impacting your actions in a positive manner.

Harmonious relationships, where love keeps elevating, are deeply supported and, in many cases, made possible by the cultivation of self-awareness. Self-awareness is initially the gift you give yourself, but it automatically expands your capacity so that you can show up for others in a more supportive and genuine way.

THE UNDERESTIMATED POWER OF PERSONAL HEALING

There is an intrinsic and undeniable connection between the relationship you have with your own emotions and how well you will be able to show up for the emotions of those you love. *If you run from your own tension, you will lack the experience to show up for the tension of others.* Self-exploration and self-transformation give you the education you need to improve your capacity to be with another person through good times and tough times.

Turning inward also shows you one of the innate follies

of human existence. Nothing will ever be flawless, and no matter how hard you try, mistakes will be made. Seeing that in your own history and not running away from that truth helps you build compassion for yourself that ultimately translates to compassion for others. You have seen yourself falter and commit actions that you later regret, or be completely misunderstood even when you are well-intentioned. You see how easy it is to get things wrong and how perfection is not attainable; this becomes a major point of growth once you allow this truth to lighten your judgment of other people when they make mistakes. If you yourself are not perfect, how can you expect others to be?

This opening of compassion allows for humility to enter, and it creates space for patience. These are qualities that can help you develop peace within yourself, and they are gifts you can give to those you interact with. The inner work that you do to heal yourself and grow is not just for your peace and progress—these are qualities that you can take with you into any situation with other human beings.

This is why personal healing is underestimated in its ability to improve our capacity to connect and care for others. Modern society is still grappling with the mass scale of trauma (according to the World Health Organization, approximately 70 percent of adults worldwide have experienced trauma), but the fact is that real healing is possible. Healing yourself—through therapy, psychiatry, meditation, or some form of effective practice—is thankfully becoming widely adopted into daily culture. It is becoming normal to meditate or to have a therapist, and this is a good sign that people today are taking their mental health and mental development seriously. Most of the attention to this work revolves around improving yourself or alleviating your mental burdens for the sake of your own inner peace. Though this work can transform you at the individual level, it also has a massive impact on how you relate to others. The ripple effect is tremendous.

I found this myself when I started meditating; not only did my mind slowly become lighter and more peaceful but all my relationships started to become more easeful and balanced. The energy I was bringing to interactions was more full of love and calmness, and others could feel this. Between Sara and me, as we continued on our meditation path, we found that we didn't need to walk on eggshells as much around each other because we were more understanding. In the past, a small thing like forgetting about a doctor's appointment would become a full-blown argument about responsibility and not respecting the other's time, but now, we may still get upset about it for a few minutes but it is accepted as a mistake and we both own our part and discuss how we can handle things better in the future.

One of the major signs of progress when you are in the process of healing yourself is how the experience of being alone changes. When being alone transitions from moments where you are intentionally diverting yourself by consuming information, like staring at the television or scrolling on your phone, to being able to be by yourself without looking for any distraction, then you know you are headed in a great direction. Letting yourself simply be is not only a sign of inner strength, but it also demonstrates the qualities of patience and self-awareness. Naturally, some people enjoy alone time more than others, but if your alone time can make space for being without distraction then this is a sign of emotional maturity. I'm naturally an extrovert and spent a lot of my teens and twenties running away from myself by always seeking to be in social settings. I didn't realize it at the time, but I was trying to avoid all the anxiety and sadness I had accumulated. But as I focused on my growth and self-development I naturally started enjoying and appreciating alone time much more.

Another important thing to consider is that even if you haven't gone through intense heartbreak or trauma, there is still room for you to become closer to yourself. Even if you have lived a beautiful and overall calm life, there are still going to be moments when you experience hardship, or where your emotions feel intense, or times when the outcome of life is in total contrast to what you desire. These moments of difficulty leave their marks on the mind and over time they make us a little more defensive and slightly less open. When we experience these hardships repeatedly, they ultimately become blocks that leave us feeling tense and heavy, and they stop us from deeply connecting with other people.

The hurts you have felt can easily become walls that stop you from being able to fully embrace another human being. The same defensive patterns that were helping you survive during a difficult time can reappear during externally peaceful moments. What helped you survive in the past can stop you from loving someone well in the present. A lot of healing revolves around letting go, and for a lot of people letting go of the past means softening in the present. This means intentionally putting your guard down and reminding yourself that emotional intimacy and connection is not a space of danger but instead an opportunity to elevate a relationship.

When you are examining if you are loving yourself well, you not only have to consider the internal dynamic of how you relate to your emotions and history, but you also have to honestly examine how you treat yourself in daily life. Loving yourself well will manifest in your intentional self-care. The way you treat yourself can have a positive or negative impact on any potential relationship.

THE ART OF SAYING YES AND NO

If you want to help others, if you want to serve the world and make it your life's mission to do good acts, then you have no other option but to make sure that you are taking good care of yourself. Your compassion for others can sometimes be so strong that you forget to ask yourself what you need and to make time for your personal revitalization. Forgetting about yourself can leave you in an unbalanced and potentially dangerous position where you push yourself into a deep level of exhaustion. Caring for others is beautiful and noble, but so is doing what you need to personally thrive. To be the best version of yourself you need to be kind to others and simultaneously give yourself what you need to flourish. It is not one or the other—it is absolutely possible to be a caring person and not totally deplete yourself in the process.

Be mindful and create systems that help you live as the best version of yourself. Be attentive and make sure that you are not overly exerting yourself. Be intentional and do what you need to keep your tank full. Having restorative practices so that you do not burn out or fall out of balance is one of the best ways to love yourself well.

Saying yes too often to the demands or requests of others can create a situation where you are burning too much of your energy. It is valuable to be kind, but not at the expense of your well-being. Knowing how much you can say yes to and actively saying no to anything that doesn't align with your intuition is needed in our fast-paced world. Being honest with yourself about what is important helps you focus your energy on your most significant goals, and it helps you show up with vitality for the people you care about the most.

It takes a lot of strength to say no and much of that strength comes from staying committed to not being a people pleaser. Sometimes there is the tendency to err too far on the side of kindness and you end up becoming overly accommodating, and other times the mind may contain patterns from childhood that stem from the fear of abandonment and cause you to crave the false security of making others happy. In both instances, people-pleasing is a form of behavior that can make you lose yourself. When you focus too much on pleasing others, you forget to meet your own needs and you falter in fulfilling the practices that help you recharge your own battery. People-pleasing is a form of behavior that is far from the balanced middle path—making sure that others get what they want from you, as opposed to making sure that you get what you need from yourself, can leave you severely depleted.

As you read this, it is important for the mind to arrive at a point of balance. It is exceedingly valuable to live a life of service, to be kind to those around you, to treat people well, and to help when you can. But this should be a measured lifestyle where you strive to do good for others while simultaneously making sure that you are treating yourself well. Going too far in either direction will lead to inner tension and outer friction. Only focusing on yourself can make you self-centered, and only focusing on others can lead you to dangerous levels of burnout. In the middle of the two you will find greater levels of inner peace and fulfillment.

Building a strong base of inner thriving is not easy. It requires a strong intention that gives your life a clear trajectory to move in. Focusing on yourself and doing what you need to do to be healthy, happy, and fulfilled is a new endeavor that the healing generation, those of us alive today who are actively healing the hurt, trauma, and counterproductive habit patterns that we carry, is currently undertaking. Staying committed to your inner thriving is something that is slowly becoming a cultural norm. Really this is a massive movement toward greater self-awareness and building practices around what you have learned about yourself to help you shine brighter in life.

Hard truth:

Your relationship with silence
will reflect how at home you feel
within your own mind and body.

If you need to constantly
get away from yourself,
there is unprocessed pain within you
that needs attention and care.

How you treat yourself in your mind is visible in the way you treat the people you encounter in daily life. Your inner world is constantly shaping your outer world and that includes the way you speak and act. When a person demonstrates unwarranted rudeness, hostility, anger, and roughness, it is a sign that their mind is a volatile place, a home without peace. The turbulence in their mind is spilling over and reaching for whoever is nearest. Often, when an individual is locked into a mode of hyper-defensiveness, as if life were a battle, this means there is a lot of unresolved trauma and old pain that has created layers of thick conditioning. This makes it hard to produce actions outside of the heavily tangled habit patterns that they picked up while trying to survive. *You can only give what you have, but that does not mean that we are all stuck as we are.* The mind is mutable; it has the capacity to change. We can undo the mental weight we carry with the help of good tools and determination.

Arriving into a relationship with a base of inner thriving is one of the greatest gifts that you can give to a new partner. Having a sense of what you need to make yourself happy is quite helpful because it stops you from expecting your happiness to solely come from your partner. This is something that the healing generation is currently grappling with: We are the makers of our own happiness, and our partners can only support and add to the happiness that flows from within us. The inner thriving that you cultivate stems from the work you have done to break delusions that have been holding you back. Constantly blaming others for any tension that your mind feels, expecting a relationship to always proceed smoothly without arguments, expecting life to not have any challenges, are all misunderstandings that have created large amounts of tension in the mind. Being able to take more responsibility over your perception and the way you react to what you feel directly supports your inner thriving.

The magic happens when two people who are in the process of, or at the very least are open to, developing their own inner thriving come together as a couple and realize that the success of their relationship is dependent on the success of their personal development.

Your healing is directly seen through
the new calmness of your reactions.

You still feel sadness, anxiety, tension, etc.,
but nowhere near as intensely as before.

Eleven Attributes of Inner Thriving

1. **You make time to heal and grow.** Whether you have experienced trauma or not, everyone has gone through hard things and those moments leave marks on the mind that impact your thoughts and actions. Finding and using healing practices that work well for you can decondition the mind so that it becomes less defensive and more open to the natural flow and beauty of life.

2. **You understand how your own perception impacts your reactions and mood.** Blaming all your emotions on events and people outside of you creates a situation where you are constantly giving your power away. Taking responsibility for your mindset not only helps you grow, but it also widens your opportunities for happiness.

3. **You are intentional about who you give your time to.** You do your best to design an inner circle that is nourishing and enjoyable. What stands out is the mutual willingness to take care of one another and the motivation to help one another figure out life's challenges.

4. **You practice bringing yourself back to the present moment.** When your mind is focusing too much on the past and future and using small details to build tension-driven narratives, you can end up creating problems

where there really are none. Being able to re-center yourself so that you don't jump to conclusions can help stop you from rolling in negativity or acting rashly.

5. **You stop glorifying busy living.** You have your goals, but you realize that you can work toward them without breaking yourself in the process. There is nothing valiant about burnout. Instead, you use your energy intentionally and put in good work toward the things you love but in a balanced way.

6. **You make time to feel gratitude.** Reflecting on all the beautiful and simple things in your life that are often taken for granted will help ground you. Being able to remember all the good things and people in your life stops the mind from solely focusing on what it wants next. It is easy to flow from gratitude to joy.

7. **You stay in touch with your emotions without becoming attached to them.** It's important to acknowledge how you feel, especially when you feel heavy, but simultaneously understand that this feeling won't last forever. Not letting temporary feelings govern your actions helps you have a less tense mind.

8. **You remind yourself to slow down.** Between the things you need to take care of in daily life and the way

technology is constantly trying to get more of your attention, so much can be missed. Slow yourself down to a healthy pace so you can be present with people, nature, and the activities you love.

9. **Follow your intuition relentlessly.** Your intuition helps you grow, leads you to your best life, and helps you make your deepest aspirations come true. Paying attention to what direction it's telling you to go in can help unfold the next chapter of your life.

10. **You live with gentleness and kindness.** You try to do good things for others, but in a balanced way so that you don't exhaust yourself. Having a giving nature and treating people well directly supports your inner peace.

11. **You always stay open to learning and growing.** You understand that you are not perfect, and you have the humility needed to continue evolving. Knowledge is ever expanding, which means there is always more to understand.

One of the best boundaries you can have
is simply not letting other people's energy
bring down your emotions.

Living in your peace even when you
come across those who want you to
join them in their storm
is a sign of deep maturity.

THE DEFINITION OF HAPPINESS

Without a proper definition, happiness will always feel elusive and unattainable. Happiness can seem like an opaque goal until you realize that what you are actually striving for is a mixture of peace and joy.

On the road to happiness many get sidetracked by thinking that what they are looking for is pleasure. Confusing happiness with pleasure becomes problematic because the craving for pleasure builds a lot of tension in the mind and it keeps the mind focused on external things. This idea makes you think that what you need is outside of you. Even when you get what you want there is always more to crave, it is a never-ending and completely dissatisfying habit pattern. Jim Carrey once said, "I think everybody should get rich and famous and do everything they ever dreamed of so they can see that it's not the answer."

After a certain amount of reflection, the insight arises that happiness is not about what you can get, it's an internally cultivated mindset. By examining your own past, you see that the distance between you and happiness has been created by the intensity of your reactions and the turbulence in your mind, both of which are internal dynamics that can shatter your enjoyment of good things that are trying to come your way or even of the things that are right in front of you. If your mind is not in a good place, it will not be able to accept the gifts that life is trying to give you.

To build a mindset that allows happiness in, you need to develop the quality of non-reactiveness. Life is generally uncontrollable, and it is not possible to live without challenges, so eventually unwanted things and tough situations will appear. Being able to create space in your mind where you can recognize something as undesirable without reacting to it intensely or suppressing it not only helps you deal with it better, but it also keeps you connected to your peace. Not blindly reacting literally allows space for peace to exist in your mind. The less you react, the more peace you have.

Similarly, for joy to exist, you need to cultivate your sense of presence. If you are disconnected from what is happening within you and from what is right in front of you, then it will not be possible to experience the true depths of joy. Being able to spend more time in the present moment and give those you are interacting with more of your genuine attention opens the possibility for more joy to arise within you.

Both peace and joy and their counterparts, non-reactiveness and present moment awareness, all stem from a particular quality of mind, equanimity. When the mind is balanced and steady, when it is taking in the world without clinging to it, when it is simply observing without judging, the mind is in a state of equanimity. The door to access the full beauty of life and the wisdom of the universe is opened by equanimity.

Goal:

Not letting the emotional
turbulence of other people
make you lose sight of
keeping your mood the
way you want it to be.

To be truly happy, equanimity has to be part of the equation. The definition of happiness is the peace and joy you feel from having an equanimous mind.

Changing your external environment, such as removing yourself from toxic situations or switching jobs or cities, can be really helpful, but nothing can deliver as great an impact in your life as changing the internal environment of your mind and heart. You have to remind yourself of this truth repeatedly on your journey because the mind does not like taking responsibility for itself, it is inclined to see all problems as external. If you take on the goal of building peace within yourself, that means you will need to focus on building three essential qualities: self-awareness, non-reactiveness, and compassion. Self-awareness is needed to stay attuned to the way your emotions change and to not allow the narratives that are built around tension to take control. Non-reactiveness helps you slow down during difficult moments so you can ask yourself how you genuinely want to show up instead of just reacting defensively. Compassion is necessary so that you can be gentler with yourself and others. Strengthening these internal qualities will help you more smoothly ride the ups and downs of life.

Reflection Questions

- What are three important things you have learned about yourself since you started building your self-awareness?
- What are you attached to?
- In what ways does your past impact the way you show up in your present life?
- How has your past shaped your present-day goals?
- Are there any emotions that you are afraid of feeling?

chapter 3

How to Thrive

Living a life where you genuinely feel like you are thriving is a very common goal. The hard part is creating the conditions for your own inner thriving. What you need to be the best version of yourself, to deeply evolve and let go of the hard parts of your past, can be worlds apart from what someone else needs.

When it comes to being in a relationship, it also seems clear that being the best version of yourself, where contentment and joy are available to you and where you understand what you need to do to create your own happiness, is important for the success of the partnership. Making yourself happy is much more long-lasting and effective than looking for someone to make you happy. The happiness, peace, and compassion that you are able to bring into the relationship will help uplift the harmony that you two create.

To be able to thrive within yourself, you need to find the right practice that will undo the dense patterning that keeps bringing your past into the present. That heavy emotional material that we all carry in our subconscious keeps our perspectives cloudy and it creates distance between us and ourselves and us and the ones we hope to love well.

There are already a multitude of practices in the world that have helped an enormous number of people so there is no need to reinvent the wheel. *Your mission is to find a practice that is challenging, but not overwhelming.* Something that can genuinely help you become stronger and address your past and unhelpful patterns, without pushing you too far too quickly. Finding the sweet spot of allowing yourself to feel the discomfort of developing the qualities that you need to improve your life and simultaneously feeling supported by the practice and community is a difficult but worthwhile mission. Reckoning with the emotional history that has been unobserved deep within your mind and heart is not an easy task. But you can find the balance by pushing yourself without knocking yourself down: If the past is coming up too strongly with the modality that you are trying and it makes you feel unbalanced or is simply too much, then that practice is not right for you at this moment in time.

Personal growth is meant to be a sustainable and long-term journey. The key word here is *sustainable;* you need to find a rhythm where you are evolving without causing yourself more discomfort than is necessary. Again, there are a wide variety of techniques that can help, Western modes of therapy, Eastern methods of meditation (there are a vast number of meditation traditions that each have unique approaches and understandings of the human mind), journaling, introspection, psychiatry, somatic healing exercises, breathwork, spending time in nature, the simple act of not running away from your emotions, even fitness routines and healthy modes of eating can become a great aid in balancing the mind. These are all methods that can help an individual, but it is important to not clump them into one box and see them all as the same—some can reach very deep layers of the mind, others less so. What matters is that you find something that feels right for you and that you use your courage to take steps forward. You will also know a technique or therapy is right for you if your intuition is clearly agreeing that this is worth your time.

Your intuition is exceedingly valuable in finding the tool that is right for you because you will notice that people have different ways of activating their self-love and self-care. If someone that you trust recommends something to you, it is a good sign that what they are doing is giving them results, but that does not necessarily mean that it is right for you. Especially for those who have gone through serious trauma or have experienced moments of mental imbalance in their lives, there are tools and methods out there for you to heal, but you have to tread carefully so that you do not overwhelm yourself once you start going inward. When it comes to deep healing, slow and steady wins the race.

Upholding two priorities
can radically improve your life:

Relentlessly trusting your intuition
with big life decisions.

Intentionally spending time with kind
people who are open to growth.

TWELVE LESSONS FROM TWELVE YEARS OF SERIOUS MEDITATION

The amazing thing about the time we live in is that today there are a bountiful number of modalities that can help you transform your life. Even within my own circle, I have seen family and friends benefit greatly from different forms of therapy, psychiatry, meditation, and lifestyle changes that build greater self-awareness. Solutions are out there, the challenge is finding something that clicks with your intuition, meets you where you are, and helps you get genuine benefits that help transform your behaviors for the better.

I feel fortunate that I was able to find what works for me when I was still very young. Thanks to my good friend Sam, I learned about a style of Vipassana meditation taught by S. N. Goenka that fit my conditioning perfectly; it helped me develop the qualities that I was seriously lacking. It helped give my life direction and placed me on a path that leads to freedom. Explicitly, freedom from the suffering we cause ourselves by unconsciously reacting and incessantly craving.

The biggest thing I have gotten from these twelve years of delving deeply into meditation is balance. The mind will jump from extreme to extreme unless you train it to understand subtlety. It will crave instead of developing conscious goals, it will hate instead of having compassion and building boundaries, it will try to control everything instead of embracing change. All the long meditation retreats I have been to and my daily meditation practice have helped me greatly. I still have much to learn and to let go of, but I can tell the time and effort I have put in has been worth it because my mind is lighter than before and it reacts with less intensity than it used to.

The following are twelve lessons I have learned from twelve years of serious meditation:

1. **Pain spreads through the web of humanity.** Those who cause hurt have been hurt. Hurt is passed down from one person to another. People who learn to heal themselves are points in the web of humanity where hurt is decreased and where it is less likely for new hurt to spread to another person. Having a mindset where you do your best to not harm those who cross your path makes the world a more peaceful place.

2. **Ego and the sense of self are not fundamentally real.** Our sense of self is created by the rapid movements of the mind. Division and hierarchy are mental constructs. Being attached to our sense of self is an attachment to an illusion. Instead of living from a place of ego, live from a place of compassion for yourself and all beings. Living from compassion is a road that leads to thriving; living from ego leads to repeating your past and

remaining in a survivalist mentality. Ego also leads to excessive blaming where you try to reason out how things are never your fault.

3. **Surround yourself with people who have the qualities you want to develop.** This will make your growth process easier because your friend group will have a culture that promotes the qualities you are actively building. Being around people who inspire you can help you feel energized to continue onward with your goals. Building your own habits helps of course, but you don't have to do everything alone. Being around friends who are moving in the same direction you want to move in will propel you forward more quickly.

4. **Your future is created by your present actions.** The energy you are putting out into the world is also formed by your actions. If you want to change your life, you need to take a serious look at the actions that are shaping it. Use the power of choice to intentionally design what your future looks like. In the present moment is where your power lies. Your past is influencing the way you are perceiving the present; be aware that your perception is trying to get you to react in the ways you did before. It takes intentional practice to break from the past and fully embrace the present as it is.

5. **Make your compassion boundless.** Intentionally living your life so that you are not trying to harm others and actively working on expanding your compassion for all beings will directly support your inner peace. A mind that hates and acts on ill will naturally struggles. When you deeply understand the power of love, you will see that no one is your enemy.

6. **Having boundaries will help you grow.** Knowing what is not for you and not being influenced by others to partake in things that weigh down your mind will support you in cultivating the best version of yourself. Skillfully speaking up for yourself, being mindful of your own capacity, saying no when it feels right to do so, and listening to your intuition about who and what you should give your energy to are ways that you define the space of your life. If you don't like someone you don't have to be around them; you can wish them the best in your mind and go your own way.

7. **Being able to see perspectives outside of your own is a sign of intelligence and mental strength.** This is a skill that helps bring harmony to interpersonal situations. When you can place yourself in other people's shoes and see things from their vantage points, it will help you understand where they are coming from, and it will stir up your compassion.

8. **You will not realize how strong you truly are until you push yourself.** Everyone is born with determination, but the way you choose to live your life can help strengthen that characteristic. You can take the strength that you build from one challenge and use it in other parts of your life. You are much stronger than you think; once you tap into that so much more becomes possible.

9. **Having a fluid sense of identity, where you allow yourself to change, leads to a happier life because you are moving with the natural flow of change as opposed to against it.** You exist because of change. When you think about who you are at the ultimate level, you are essentially the coming together of physical and mental phenomena at incredibly fast speeds—from the cellular down to the subatomic, everything about you is in motion. This should inspire you to allow your preferences, likes, and dislikes to evolve over time. Don't be attached to the old you, let the new you emerge.

10. **Trying to control everything is a recipe for great mental tension.** The attachments in your mind will manifest as attempts to control things in your daily life. Understanding that you can only control your own actions is necessary to establish inner peace. Of course we can influence one another but we cannot design one an-

other's lives. Let go often if you want to really know what peace feels like.

11. **Setting time and space aside so you can work on yourself is not selfish; it is actually a great gift you give to yourself and to those around you.** Seeing your life as a growth journey will require you to be aware of what you need to cultivate, and it will give you the courage to say no to other things so you can do so. There is always a trade-off, but the energy you put into working on yourself will help you be much more present, caring, and confident when you are around friends and family.

12. **Deep inner struggle comes from having a bad relationship with change.** If you hate change, your mind will be full of tension. The entirety of reality is just one enormous river of change—fighting against that is a battle that is bound to be lost. Embracing change is the key to happiness and wisdom; it will also help you appreciate all the little things and the people in your daily life. Embracing change helps you stay in your gratitude. Embracing change helps your mind remain in its balance.

If you are looking for great advice,
close your eyes and listen to your intuition.

The people who love you can give you
good advice but ultimately you know your
situation and your goals better than anyone else.

Get comfortable leading yourself.

HEALING IS POSSIBLE

All my years of meditation, the hours I have put in on the cushion, have given me an undeniable and undoubtable confidence in the fact that human beings can heal themselves. Change at the deepest level is possible—negative habits that lead to mental tension and bad choices do not have to last forever, and with intention they can be unbound and new happiness-affirming habits can take their place.

I know this from firsthand experience because I suffered deeply from anxiety, sadness, and fear when I was in my late teens and early twenties. This intensity would weigh down my mind and make me look at myself and the world through a negative lens; it was a heaviness that became so unbearable that I started using drugs and alcohol to avoid my inner tension. I also always tried to be around other people to avoid the heavy emotions that plagued me most when I was alone. These coping mechanisms that I picked up from the culture around me led me down a dark path. On a daily basis I would choose inebriating my mind to avoid the difficult feelings in my body. After years of coping through intoxicants, my body began to fail me; it felt broken, tender, and incredibly weak. One night in particular, I almost lost my life when I took too many drugs and my heart lost its rhythm for a few hours. My heart felt like it was going to explode. In that moment I felt like my time on earth was ending, like my life was slipping away as I lay on the floor crying and trying to will myself to stay alive. I had been too full of fear and shame to seek help. Fortunately, I was able to pick myself up after and start a new life. I know that not everyone gets a second chance. When I later described what happened to a doctor she told me it sounded like I had a mild heart attack. I was incredibly lucky that wasn't the end—it actually turned out to be the beginning.

After those years of focusing on intoxicating my mind so that I would not have to pay attention to any of the tough emotions that were passing through my body, I was unfamiliar with simply being. All I had known for those years was taking some type of drug or alcohol to help me exist, to facilitate life and my interactions with other people. After committing to stopping all the hard drugs, I realized that I was a stranger in my own mind and body, that I needed to get to know myself and the only way to do that was to start telling myself the hard truth. I finally accepted the sadness, anxiety, and fear that I had been constantly running away from, and whenever they would appear again, I would challenge myself to feel them instead of running back into my old bad habits.

As my body got healthier and I started befriending my emotions, I came across Vipassana meditation. That was when the healing became so deep that it started introducing me to freedom. I was absolutely wowed by the fact that meditating was helping my mind become more present, calmer, and less rigid. My mind and body genuinely felt lighter. I was shocked that real healing was possible; when I was growing up no one had told me that we don't have to live forever with the mental afflictions that we acquire in life. The fact that I was able to unload the past and reduce the intensity of my rough emotional reactions without any suppression, simply by observing them as they arose and passed away, was the beginning of a personal paradigm shift for me.

In my own example and in the lives of friends, I have seen that when you set your mind to overcoming inner turmoil and you combine that energy with a proven tool that can give you results, the potential for positive change becomes massive. I have seen countless friends become more peaceful and skillful because of meditation. Some of them used the technique I practice and others found great techniques in other traditions. One of the best things to happen to me is getting to witness that there is no one way to heal, that everyone can't use the same technique, that individuals need to find what works for them. Even outside of seeing many different types of meditation help people change their lives, the same goes for various forms of Western therapy. I have heard so many amazing stories of people finding the right therapist or modality that helped them let go of an old pattern and bring more understanding into their lives.

If you are wondering who
your people are, they are
the ones who make your
heart feel seen and your
nervous system feel calm.

Yes, it's that simple.

We live in an incredibly imperfect and unbalanced time; you could spend hours and hours detailing what is wrong with the world, but the one thing that always gives me hope is that millions of people are actively healing themselves in our current era. It genuinely feels like a healing generation is rising. This is historically unprecedented; healing is something that was available before in many cultures, but it was usually kept within the smaller communities. But now that the world is globalized, the techniques that greatly produce results are gaining popularity and they are slowly spreading and becoming more accessible. As people keep reducing their trauma and building better habits, they will be inspired to help spread these tools. One day healing may even become a human right. All who suffer should be supported in accessing the tools they need to release the tension in their minds.

THE STUDENT MENTALITY AND SPIRITUAL ARROGANCE

With all these lessons, the most important thing I learned over these years of serious meditation is maintaining the mindset of a student. I know that I have much to learn and that teachers come in different ways, through the random people we meet, the books we pick up, and the formal teachers that give us the tools that we use to develop our minds and hearts. Honestly, seeing myself as a student keeps things simple and it helps me see that I can grow in wisdom, that I have more to let go of, and that I would benefit from more self-awareness.

Especially when it comes to growth-related pursuits, the experiences that we accumulate should not get twisted into arrogance. The ego is quite sneaky and it will grab anything to make itself bigger. The ego is always looking for ways to create divisions and hierarchy. Part of the energy that keeps the ego together is fear, thus it will look for any reason to see others as less than. If it thinks that it knows something that others don't, it will use that information to create a feeling of superiority.

Reaffirming within yourself that you still have much to learn and that there are many people in the world you can learn from will support the humility that is needed to truly blossom in your happiness and freedom. Humility is one of the primary characteristics that gives stability to your inner peace. Humility requires a certain degree of inner balance where you have confidence in yourself, but you are also happy to hear the wisdom and experience of others in the hope that it may bring clarity to your own path.

If the ego is growing, then your freedom is shrinking. Spiritual arrogance can become a giant hindrance. The truths that you encounter can be life-changing, but that doesn't mean you have everything figured out or that you should give yourself the title of teacher. One thing to be wary of when seeking a teacher is someone who exudes this type of "I know everything" arrogance. Arrogance is a form of mental thickness and density, it makes the mind inflexible and it heavily clouds perception—someone who is openly telling you they know everything most likely has a lot to learn themselves.

The wisest people I have ever encountered in my life were also the humblest people and the kindest. The two people I think of as my teachers have extensive backgrounds in meditation. One has taken meditation seriously for more than fifty years and the other for over thirty years. Both of them move through life with a mindset that is eager to serve others. They are selfless, uninterested in fame, dedicated to helping people, and they do their best to treat all people as compassionately as possible. Their peace is evident, and their humility is felt through their actions. Neither of them sought to become meditation teachers; instead they were asked to serve as meditation teachers by those who taught them.

There is something quite special in the example of the Buddha. After his enlightenment, he did not immediately start teaching. He spent a few weeks continuing to meditate and walk around the area of Bodh Gaya in northern India. During that time, he reflected on what he understood and enjoyed the peace of true egolessness and the freedom that comes when one extinguishes the fire of craving. After some time, a being named Brahma Sahampati came down to speak with the Buddha and asked him to not keep his knowledge and the path of freedom to himself, he asked him to teach in the hopes that others may also be free. The Buddha, even though he knew the path to freedom was difficult to teach, realized that he should do so out of compassion, but he only allowed himself to teach after he was asked to do so by another. There is an element of humility there that is quite inspiring.

Seeing yourself as a perpetual student keeps the mind open and agile. Developing arrogance closes the mind to further expansion. If it is really your mission to learn and grow, if happiness is one of your goals, then you will have to do your best to set aside the pompousness of ego. There is knowledge out there that you do not even know exists. Information that can help you improve your life and mind. To be able to acquire that which is outside your realm of insight, the mind needs to intentionally break down the walls that arrogance tries to create.

ON SLOWING DOWN

The power of slowing down is underestimated because of its simplicity, but it can be one of the most useful tools in your journey forward.

Everything feels like it is moving lightning fast—social media, technology, news. We quickly jump from one new thing to another. The speed of everything is exhausting; this can cause stress and anxiety because our environment is never still, it is in constant flux.

The structure of society that we form in our minds and

the views we lean on that bring stability to our identities are constantly being re-formed and challenged. What we know is always morphing and what we think we should know is ever expanding.

Beyond the inner tension that is caused by the relentless speed, there is also the fact that quickness makes it hard to take a good look at something. Because we are collectively jumping from one thing to the next, it becomes easier to adopt the opinions of others as our own instead of slowing down to learn more and examine what is happening, or even simply admitting that we don't know enough to make an informed opinion. We innately want to stay with the herd so that we don't get left behind, but this may come at the price of failing to expand our understanding and refine our critical lens.

The simplest thing you can do
for your mental health is move
at your natural speed.

Don't feel rushed by the people around you.
Take your time responding to texts and emails.

Everything doesn't need an immediate solution.
Don't let technology boss you around.

It takes courage to slow down and form a clear view of the world. It takes valiant energy to live in your power and hit the brakes so you can stay aligned with what is important to you. If you want to be your own person, it will require you to move at your own pace. If you stick to the pace of those around you, the potential of losing yourself becomes greater.

Slowing down is how you ground yourself. It is how you reconnect with your peace and intuition. Slowing down helps you understand yourself and other people. Slowing down opens the door to deeper learning. It is how you reaffirm the way you want to show up in the world. Slowing down is necessary if you want to live intentionally. It is the only way you can make sure that you are moving in the right direction.

The world is changing fast, especially technologically. The speed at which we receive information and the sheer quantity of opinions online is daunting. Forcing ourselves to have an opinion on every single matter that arises is unrealistic; it takes a lot of time to process unbiased information and build an educated view on a topic. To slow ourselves down, so we can simply listen, ponder, and learn more about different global situations, feels hard when the internet is begging us to jump to conclusions. Even so, if we want to live in our power, we need to slow down, especially when it feels like the world is moving fast. There is nothing wrong with saying, "I actually want to learn more about what is going on before I give my opinion." Asking questions to learn more is another great way to participate without jumping to conclusions. The speed at which technology moves is anxiety inducing and it can set us up to think frantically, to jump from extreme to extreme. This means that the tools we use to develop our inner peace and well-being are more important than ever. To be able to deal with the chaos of the world, we need to consistently tend to our inner harmony. To do that, it is essential to hold our healing as a top priority.

Of course, taking the time to understand every little thing is not possible and we can't always grind to a halt, but bringing awareness to the fact that everything is moving quickly can help us intentionally slow down when we feel overstimulated or during important moments. The key skill to develop is being intentional about our attention and giving ourselves time to develop a more well-rounded perspective. *Being able to slow down when we want to or need to is a reflection of our maturity.*

THE POWER OF FLOWING INSTEAD OF FORCING

Trying to stay the same is painful and trying to mold everything to the way you desire is impossible.

The overarching truth of reality is that it is always moving forward. Nothing is static, nothing stays still, everything is in a constant state of flow. Every level of existence in our universe essentially creates a river of change. Never is the river the same, nor will it ever be fully predictable or controllable.

The river of change does not create a destiny of chaos or aimlessness, nor does it take our power away. This motion of impermanence simply creates a balance where we can express ourselves through our thoughts, words, and actions in the present moment, but it disallows any individual from having total control over reality—this creates a situation where, whether we like it or not, we will have to learn to let go of our craving for a certain outcome. Everything will not work out the way we want it to.

Change is also trying to gift us a lesson in letting our sense of identity morph as we go through the vicissitudes of life. Keeping your preferences and perspectives the same over years and decades is not possible or logical. Your mind, consciously and unconsciously, is constantly processing new information that over time shifts how you see yourself and the world. Even if these shifts are small and initially unnoticeable, you will eventually see them as your likes and dislikes begin to differ and your actions start representing your new evolution. Trying to stay the same is an attempt to swim against the river of change. It requires a bit of delusion and a lot of effort to genuinely believe that you don't change.

Some people from your past
will hang on to a version of you
that no longer exists.

Years of experience, growth, and
overcoming challenges cannot help
but change you.

If you like who you are now and finally
feel happy in your mind and life,
that is ultimately what matters most.

If you intentionally try to observe reality, you will notice it is inviting you to embrace a mindset of flow. Not only should you allow your identity to flow as you learn more about yourself and the world, but you should do your best to flow through life as opposed to trying to control every possible outcome.

It is important to practice this without going to extremes: You should have goals and intentionally build your life through your actions, this is good for you, but letting go of controlling every little thing will help you think more clearly and have more peace. Even with big setbacks, being able to process and then move forward, rather than getting bowled over by an undesirable outcome, is a great skill. Similarly, having a sense of values that function like an anchor for your identity is useful because this will help you relate with the world and the people around you. Values can function like a filter that assists you in deciding who and what is or is not for you. A mindset of flow is not about being actionless and utterly amorphous, it is about living an active life while remembering that change is something to embrace instead of fight.

Flowing instead of forcing is easier when you intentionally let go of attachments. The mind creates a lot of attachments quickly; it will crave certain outcomes over others, and it will try to make them happen. The problem is that sometimes what we want to happen is far outside our realm of control, especially when what we crave involves other people. Attachment can lead into the attempt to control others, and this only results in removing the freedom and joy from our relationships. At best you can give advice or let others know your wishes, but you cannot control how others act.

When you intentionally try to flow through life, you do your best to be clear in your communications, but you remember that the true flourishing of any relationship requires alignment in your commitments instead of forcing things to go your way all the time. Making attachments is like trying to throw anchors into the river of change except this is a river that has no bottom, the anchors will not help you get the outcomes you crave, and each one will weigh you down more and make your mind feel heavier.

For many, flowing instead of forcing requires a real shift and an alteration of personal life philosophy. We normally grow up with attachment and we have to teach ourselves to let go more and more often. Letting go is in no way easy, but we choose this path because it is the only one that results in genuine happiness, inner peace, and the type of wisdom that helps you be free.

ON GROWTH AND KINDNESS

Selfishness is a misconception in the wellness world.

When you decide to embrace your evolution, you will undoubtedly begin to make different life decisions. Your actions will start becoming more aligned with how you aspire to show up in the world, your preferences will slowly shift, and what you want from your interactions with other people will resemble the authenticity that you are developing within yourself. Since you are working on creating connection within yourself, you will seek deeper connections with those around you.

Along the way, there will be people in your life who do not approve of the way you are changing and others who applaud your growth. A tough aspect about a period of transformation is that you cannot control other people's perceptions; for their own reasons and because of past conditioning, some may be taken off guard by your changes and may even resist them. This can be especially true if you are experimenting with boundaries, new healing modalities, making new friends, and testing out new worldviews to see which fits you best.

As you grow, it is important to keep in mind that kindness still matters. Kindness to yourself and others is a sign of great maturity and inner development. Culturally, in the wellness world, there is a trendy misconception that personal growth makes you selfish, but that is far from the truth and genuinely counterproductive.

Growth and self-love are not meant to make your ego bigger. In truth, developing more compassion for others is a sign that your self-love is real. After spending time with yourself, examining your mind, old hurts, and past conditioning, you should start to see how your mind works and how it impacts your daily life. For many, this experience of understanding yourself helps you see that you are not the only one suffering; others are also having a hard time moving through the same spectrum of emotions.

Self-love and growth will naturally ask you to refocus your attention on yourself to make sure that you have established the proper systems and habits in your life to help you move forward. It takes time to learn how to treat yourself well so that you can function at a happier and more optimal level, but this is quite different from becoming egocentric. *Seeing yourself as more important than others, treating others harshly, quickly excommunicating friends, or rapidly labeling those you don't like as toxic is not conducive to life-changing growth.*

An important part of growing is realizing that nothing is ever going to be perfect, even in our closest relationships. Relationships are bound to have manageable degrees of conflict that if held properly can become points of understanding that bring you closer together. Conflict resolution is an essential part of being in any relationship or community. Having an argument does not necessarily mean the situation is toxic. Over time, running from conflict will decrease your chances of developing healthy and nourishing connections. Granted, this does not excuse abusive behavior that is truly harmful, and in these cases it is certainly needed to create space between you and that person.

What you should strive for is balance.

Treat yourself well and simultaneously be kind to others. Help people when you can but be mindful to not exhaust yourself or burn out. Give while also making sure that you have enough for yourself. Going to extremes, one way or the other, will create mental tension and struggle.

The reason wellness has picked up so much steam and is now such a large movement is because people seriously want to transform their lives for the better, but we need to make sure that we don't go the other way where we solely care for ourselves and feel fine about treating others harshly. If your freedom is growing, then your ego is shrinking.

Even when you intentionally try to take care of yourself and be kind to others, you are not going to get it right every time. Others may still see you in a negative light because you are not behaving or doing things in the way that they prefer. These are uncontrollable factors that are part of life. Even so, a point of inner victory is attained when you have compassion for yourself and others. Getting yourself to this mindset is needed to experience true inner peace.

Ten Reflections That Will Help You Succeed

1. **Give yourself time to envision your own future.** Let yourself see what comes next. Don't place limitations on yourself when you think about your next chapter. Let your mind reach far and allow your sight to be oriented

by your deepest aspirations. Above all, what do you want life to feel like? Before you act, let your mind and heart create a clear direction for you.

2. **The closest relationships in your life are a direct reflection of your relationship with your own emotions.** When you can be with and embrace the tumultuousness that may temporarily arise within you, this strengthens your capacity to give your loving attention to someone you care for when they are going through something difficult. If you find distance between yourself and someone you love, ask yourself, "Is there a way to become closer to myself so that I can deepen my connection with them?"

3. **You have lived with your mind long enough to know that heavy emotions will sometimes cloud your perception.** You will not be able to see yourself well when your mind is moving through an emotional storm. A large enough storm will make everything look dark and cloudy. Don't let a temporary moment of mental heaviness become a blame game where you start judging yourself harshly.

4. **If you want to create more harmony with those you are closest to, you should widen your channel of communication so that you are both clear about**

how you would like your happiness to be supported. Don't let what would add to your joy be a mystery to each other. Checking in with your partner, as well as friends and family members, about how you would like to show up for each other will help remove confusion.

5. **Perception is memory combined with evaluation.** Whatever you encounter in the present moment will be measured according to what it most resembles from your past. This process moves incredibly quickly, and it makes it hard to create a fresh understanding of what is happening right in front of you. The point of this mental process is survival, but constantly seeing the present through the lens of the past will make it difficult for you to thrive. The only way to retrain the mind is by intentionally slowing down. Knowing that the mind likes to jump to judgment and putting your energy into actively taking in the present will allow you to see more of what is right in front of you.

6. **Moving at your natural speed is not only one of the best ways to rebel—it is also one of the most important ways to love yourself.** Society will try to push you into an unreasonable speed of existence, but adopting the speed of others will only cause you tension. A busy life does not automatically equal a successful life. Taking time to breathe and process your emotions is the

best way to take intentional steps forward. These mini moments of getting to know yourself will help you produce skillful actions. When you practice moving organically, you will see that rushing was hampering your ability to share your gifts with the world.

7. **Have you held your happiness in your own hands lately or have you been placing it in the hands of others?** Even though you know that the deepest foundation of happiness begins within you, it is easy to fall into old patterns where you are giving away your power. Old patterns take time to unbind. Repeatedly centering yourself around the fact that your perception can make or break your happiness will help you walk into the present moment with greater appreciation and ownership.

8. **Evaluate how much you are saying yes.** Is how often you say yes adding to your life and goals or is this merely causing exhaustion? Is each yes bringing you into alignment or making you feel greater discord? Are you saying yes from a genuine place or are you saying it out of fear of causing disappointment?

9. **Your relationship with change is a clear barometer for the amount of stress your mind carries.** If you embrace change, the ups and downs of life will cause you less tension. If you have a combative relationship

with change, then you will struggle when you repeatedly feel that much of life is outside of your control. Time and life only flow forward in the form of an ever-changing river. If your inner peace is important to you, then you need to learn to move with the current as opposed to moving against it.

10. **The more intense your reaction, the greater your level of stress and anxiety**. Others can certainly create challenges in your life, but your greatest challenge is within you. The way you react to what you feel defines the quality of your life. If you truly want to reclaim your power and build inner peace, turn your attention inward and pay attention to your mental movements. Before you can change your reactions, you must first see how much unnecessary tension you are causing yourself.

A NOTE ON BELIEVING IN YOURSELF

Many people will cross your path who will not be able to see your vision. This may make you doubt yourself or reconsider if what you are putting energy into is even worth it. The important thing is to realize that everything is not for everyone. People have different tastes, needs, and preferences and often are coming from a place of fear. The only validation for your vision that you genuinely need is that of your own intuition.

If you feel your inner compass pointing you toward a clear direction, then you can have confidence to pursue it. Having goals that are different from those of the people around you can sometimes make you feel alone or unsupported, but that is often how it is in the beginning.

Once people start seeing results, that your goal is something achievable, they are more likely to become supportive. This happens to many people who walk outside of their comfort zones and put their energy into creating something new—you must have the courage to walk the path alone if necessary and eventually others will join you.

Reflection Questions

- What does thriving mean to you?
- Do you have habits that are holding you back from thriving?
- What would you like to change about your daily routine?
- What does your ideal life look like?
- What is one of your biggest victories?

chapter 4

Where We Stumble

The biggest challenge to inner peace and inner thriving is attachment. In this chapter and throughout this book, attachment will directly refer to the ancient understanding that craving for something or someone to exist in a particular way is a source of misery. This is a central teaching of the Buddha, and it has ramifications that are incredibly relevant in our modern times. Not only does attachment weigh down the mind of an individual, but as we will later explore, attachment can be a corrosive element that can bring down and potentially break a relationship.

Attachment is a deep form of inflexibility. It is a craving that runs so deep in the mind that it creates tension. While you are dreaming about what you crave and trying to preserve the things you have already attained, the mind is creating a tense atmosphere for itself that directly blocks peace from arising. Attachment also holds a very narrow perspective, which struggles to see anything other than its own desire.

The mind is tilted toward the craving for control; evolutionarily this makes sense because of the inner impulse to survive. Not only is our deep human programming geared toward survival mode, but our childhoods and life experiences will often strengthen that programming as we experience varying degrees of hurt and trauma. Life is not easy and in the process of surviving, we harden. Not only do our hearts become less open, because we fear that no one will be able to receive our vulnerability, but our minds become more focused on expanding what we can control.

If life is hard, shouldn't we strive to control as much as possible to keep ourselves safe? That seems like the logical direction we should take, but seeking to control quickly backfires because there are far too many factors involved in each situation. It is impossible to control the multiplicity of possibilities and variables that go into creating each moment and every individual. Seeking control is like falling for the classic mirage of water in a desert. Control is an illusion that we trick ourselves into believing. *As wise people have repeatedly realized through self-observation, the only things you can control are your own actions.*

Striving to control keeps your attention outward, always seeking an external factor you can impact that will bring you peace, instead of turning your attention inward and finding peace within yourself. People often spend their entire lifetimes looking outward when the answer is within. The relentless pursuit of control keeps the mind tense and geared toward anxiety.

The drive to control is pushed along by attachment but there is an underlying misunderstanding that gives this pattern its power. We forget that we live in a river of impermanence. Even when we say we understand this truth, we still strive to create a permanent haven held together by our precise cravings within this river of impermanence. This craving to have things exist in the manner that we desire arises from our inability to fully embrace change. Impermanence is pervasive at every level of existence, and no matter how hard we may try, the river of change will always flow forward, eventually eroding everything we have created. Fundamentally, everything that exists will ultimately pass away; things, situations, and people can exist only for a finite amount of time. Trying to fight this truth is a great cause of misery.

> One day Ajahn Chah held up a beautiful Chinese teacup. "To me this cup is already broken. Because I know its fate, I can enjoy it fully here and now. And when it's gone, it's gone." When we understand the truth of uncertainty and relax, we become free.
>
> —*Jack Kornfield,* The Wise Heart

The opposite of control is teaching ourselves to live in harmony with this flow and to embrace the dynamic quality of reality. If we cannot stop change, we may as well befriend it and learn how to move with it. This is probably one of the hardest realizations to integrate into your life. Embracing change requires practice. The old habit of the mind will fight change because it fears it, but the only path toward true happiness requires you to embrace the truth of impermanence.

The fear of change is logical because change can take away the things we like, but we often fail to realize that change is the great giver of opportunity. Life itself is possible because our universe is based on motion. If everything were static, nothing would ever come into being. Because things move, we have a chance to exist, learn, and grow. Change can create hardship, but it also can create beauty and all the wondrous aspects of life that we deeply cherish.

Teaching ourselves to flow with change does not mean that we stop making decisions and that we become passive players in life. Flowing with change requires a deep understanding of balance. The goal is to accept the fact that you can't control everything while you move intentionally through your life. You use the power of your actions to work patiently and steadfastly to attain your goals and build a good life for yourself, but you simultaneously know that everything is not under your control. Ideally you will use your actions to construct, and when the wind blows, you won't be shaken and upset, instead you will assess what is lost and continue building in the direction of a life that is even better than what you had previously imagined. Knowing that setbacks will happen and doing your best to face them with tolerance and acceptance is the goal. Flowing with change requires the antithesis of attachment, which is letting go.

Going with the flow does not mean
you sit back passively and expect
everything to work out.

Going with the flow means you don't
cause yourself stress by fighting changes
that are out of your control.

CLINGING TO THE PAST

Another obstacle to inner thriving is hanging on to the past. The mind struggles with letting go and it will keep dragging the past into the present. The past may show up as solidified forms of identity that we keep clinging to because we are used to seeing ourselves in that manner. It may also show up as triggers that cause painful emotions and memories to resurface, or in relationships as old grievances reemerging even though our partner is a different person today. This is one of the main reasons why healing is such a critical component toward living your best life. Healing is done right if it teaches you how to let go. Staying attached to your own past will keep your mind heavy and clouded.

One of the most challenging obstacles in life is the ignorance we have regarding the inner workings of our own mind. Initially, impulsive reactions can feel genuine and righteous, but when you start looking inward it becomes clear that impulsive reactions often have very little to do with what is happening in the present moment. Impulsive reactions are bridges that connect whatever you are perceiving in the present with a feeling of the past. How we react and how intensely that reaction manifests through our thoughts, words, and actions is a revelation of how deeply the past still has a hold over our mind.

Hard truth:

Boundaries alone are not enough
to bring you deep inner peace.

You also need to realize how your
own reactions are causing you stress.

Before you can change your perception
you first need to be real with yourself
about how it's affecting you.

Every reaction to what you feel leaves a mark on the mind, a mark that over time becomes a pattern that hardens and makes your actions rigid. The important thing to note here is that the mind is constantly reacting to the feelings in the body. When the mind is full of thoughts of anxiety or it is running through tough memories, all the emotions that you are feeling, even though you experience them quite strongly at the mental level, are rooted and grounded in the sensations of the body. When you feel anger, there is a sensation in the body. When you feel anxiety, there is a clear sensation in the body. Passion, fear, jealousy, all of these dense emotions appear with sensations in the body.

Sensations in the body are the link between whatever the mind is experiencing and how we react. We are not actually reacting to our thoughts; we are reacting to how we feel. This was one of the great discoveries of the Buddha. The Anguttara Nikaya, one of the many collections that hold the Buddha's teachings, states, "Everything that arises in the mind is accompanied by sensation."

Even if this is not immediately evident, it is a truth that comes to life when the mind becomes sharp and subtle; through direct observation it ultimately becomes clear that the patterning of the mind that shapes our behavior starts with the way we react to our sensations.

The way we have reacted in the past has a direct impact on how we perceive reality. The mind will quickly take anything it is perceiving and match it with something that is similar to the past it has experienced. Not only will your perception match what you are experiencing, but it will evaluate it as negative or positive, something that it feels aversion toward or something that it craves.

The mind is geared toward judgment and unclear perception. The mind normally struggles to witness the present as it is because it is filtering reality through the heavily conditioned past; this creates great difficulty in daily life. Having part of your mind here and part of your mind still battling the past is a great source of inner tension. The glaring truth is that this is a struggle that is pervasive throughout humanity. If you have a mind, then much of it will be clinging to the past. Granted, the past is useful in the sense that it is informative and it can help us make sense of the world, avoid prior mistakes, and make better behavioral choices, but when we are deeply attached to the past, either through craving something in particular or by feeling the deep aversion that comes up with trauma, genuinely being in the present becomes a massive battle. This is a common difficulty and roadblock of the human experience.

Fortunately, healing is possible; ways to alleviate past trauma and hurt are becoming more widely accessible, and methods for repatterning the mind in ways that are conducive to mental clarity and good living are becoming more abundant.

Before I began meditating, I struggled with this terribly. My mind could barely sit in the present moment. It was constantly judging, reacting, and jumping between craving and aversion. Everything I witnessed was quickly filtered through my heavy past. Anytime I felt threatened, my reactions were loud and overly defensive. This was creating great tension in my relationship with Sara because my past was constantly on a mission to block a peaceful present from existing. When we would speak, I could barely listen and was too focused on my own points.

Whenever our conversations got too serious, I felt the rush of anxiety in my body and my thought patterns turned negative and defensive. Fear would fill my perspective and I would try my best to avoid responsibility. Even though we were just speaking, it felt like I was in genuine danger. This made it so that our conversations could barely break through the surface, if at all. For the first few years of our relationship, it felt as if we were stuck at the beginning, finding joy and comfort in each other's presence, but without the deeper emotional connection that comes from gifting each other our vulnerability. Little did I know at the time that to be vulnerable one has to have the strength to overcome the franticness of survival mode and defensiveness.

Meditation changed this for me because it focused directly on mental training and letting go. It taught me to befriend the present moment and to do my best to observe it objectively. Much of this involved simply bringing my attention back to what is, as opposed to letting my perception project the past onto whatever I was encountering. This repetition of intentionally moving my attention slowly cultivated my weak mental muscles. As I practiced giving attention to the present moment, I became able to listen to Sara in a more selfless manner. When hard conversations would arise, the impulse to run or be defensive was still there, but I now had the training to bring my attention back to the conversation and do my best to observe what was happening without throwing my old judgments onto the situation. Cultivating present moment awareness opened the door to deeper connection within myself and with her. *Listening takes a lot of strength, especially when you are listening to understand as opposed to listening to respond.*

The other major benefit from meditating was that for my whole life my mind had felt heavy. My reactions were so quick that I barely had any control over them. The defensive and survivalist pattern that most often manifested as sadness, anxiety, and fleeing from anything that became too emotionally difficult felt like something that had hardened into concrete. At that time, my mind felt incredibly rigid and immovable. So when I started meditating I was shocked that my mind felt a little bit lighter; there was a sudden openness that started expanding. I was especially able to see this transformation over time as I kept going to silent ten-day retreats; I would do three to four a year. I felt a major difference in my own mind and soon I started seeing that the quality of my relationship with Sara was improving. Not only did I begin appreciating her more but when difficult conversations would arise my mind started feeling like it had more possibilities than just reacting with negativity, defensiveness, or counterarguments that would simply add to the fire of the argument. This was at first a very shocking experience because I was so familiar with the old flow of events: hard topic comes up, do my best to avoid blame, defend, defend, defend, and hope the argument ends without us breaking up.

The difference came when the hard topic would come up and I could feel the defensiveness arising within my mind, but it was no longer the only option. Instead it was one possibility among a few paths I could take. It felt like my mind was able to process more than the impulsive reaction, it could see there were other more productive, genuine, and harmonizing actions that I could take. Actions such as admitting my own mistakes in a situation, taking responsibility for my part of it, apologizing, trying to genuinely understand where she was coming from or what was at the root of my mental tension, and trying to bring us closer to a solution that we both felt good about. This was not an overnight victory and in no way have we elevated arguing and handling conflict to a perfect art form, but it is definitely not the way it used to be for us. The great thing was that we took the meditation adventure together, so we were both able to feel this new mental spaciousness and novel sense of choice that could lead us to a shared space of harmony.

I like to think of the healing that happened through

meditation as lightening the load. My mind was heavy with the past and that patterned my behavior, but meditation helped weaken those reaction patterns over time. Reaction is a muscle just like peace. The more I intentionally practiced present moment awareness and objectivity, the more that heavy load of reaction weakened. The value of pausing so that you can respond as opposed to react is becoming a more popular notion, but what is commonly left out is that this requires training. It is hard to simply do it, just as it would be hard to run a marathon without any training. You have to intentionally try over and over again, literally reinforcing a new set of positive behaviors in your mind until they eventually become second nature. At first it can feel clunky and even a bit disingenuous, but you have to remind yourself that your impulsive reaction is just an echo of the past, and the way you react is not the real you.

A more genuine representation is what you intentionally choose as your action after the craving subsides. If you stay committed to developing a new you, there will eventually be a moment of victory when you realize that you were able to make a good decision for yourself that feels productive and aligned rather than robotic and past-oriented. Again, there is nothing wrong with being in touch with your past and letting it inform you, but that doesn't mean you should be living your past over and over again by reacting in the same ways that you used to. If you want to live a new and better life, keep the information from the past but let go of the negative ways you would react in the past. A world of possibility opens up when you finally start letting go. Only through healing and letting go can you choose behaviors that bring forward more vibrant living.

I healed deeply through meditation, and it became the catalyst for a more profound and invigorating relationship with Sara. But people heal in different ways, and the important thing is to embrace the fact that anyone can benefit from some degree of healing and cultivation. No one has everything figured out and we all definitely have qualities that we can improve on to help us flourish as individuals and in interpersonal situations. Just like a garden, you need to clear the land, plant the seeds, and water them patiently, while also making sure you do occasional weeding. When you practice new responses to challenging situations you are removing the weeds of past reactions and lightening the load of your mind. Your intentions to evolve are like seeds, and they must be nourished by your consistent efforts to love and care for yourself well through healing and self-development.

Even though Sara and I healed deeply through meditation and strengthened useful qualities that make life more vibrant, there was still a lot for us to learn about love. We were building foundations of peace within ourselves, but we still didn't know how to love each other well. It started with giving each other patience and our newfound ability to listen, but we realized that we needed an entirely new culture between us. We needed to develop our own practice of love.

Eleven Truths That Should Not Be Ignored

1. **If you want to connect with wisdom and the beauty of the moment, you need to move slowly.** Rushing will make you miss so much, and it is actually just a reflection of your inner agitation.

2. **The law of cause and effect is predominant in nature.** If you want a good life, focus on doing good actions as selflessly as possible. The people you help, the things you give, the kindness you emit, all of these are seeds that will bear good fruit in the future.

3. **You know your heart better than anyone else.** This means you need to act on what you know. Speak up for yourself, ask for support when needed, don't feel like you need to move at the same speed or in the same direction as everyone else.

4. **Giving away too much of your time to the requests of others will stop you from giving time to what is good and nourishing for you.** Betraying yourself is not virtuous. Constantly saying yes to please others will lead

to burnout. Say no frequently if you want to create a clear space in your life for what matters most to you.

5. **Your energy leaves an imprint on the environment that you are in and the people you are with.** Places where the Buddha and his disciples meditated twenty-six hundred years ago remain surprisingly vibrant and powerful. Your energy does not stay only with you, it moves outward and invites others to feel the same way.

6. **Trying to avoid all conflicts and arguments is not possible.** Interpersonal conflict happens because egos exist. Approaching conflict with selflessness and the goal to understand helps harmony reappear more easily.

7. **Real healing is possible, but so is real freedom.** Suffering is not eternal. With the right practices you can slowly but surely decrease the tension that exists in your mind. You can even go as far as to fully extinguish personal suffering, but this takes serious work.

8. **You don't have to be perfect to have made tremendous progress.** If you are reacting less intensely than before, if your mind feels lighter, if you are making better decisions, then you are moving in a good direction. Mistakes will happen, setbacks are common, and that is okay and natural.

9. **Everything requires balance.** Going to extremes creates needless friction. Let boldness mix with gentleness. Let your giving match your receiving. Let your striving match your relaxation. If you look with a calm mind, you will be able to find a middle path in most situations.

10. **It is exceedingly easy to take for granted the things you are surrounded by on a daily basis—your family, the food you eat, small enjoyments—but once they are gone you see how much you relied on it all and simply expected it to be there.** Be more intentional about looking around with fresh eyes to see the abundance in front of you. A major shift in attitude and perspective can be as simple as having gratitude.

11. **Be mindful of the story you are writing in your mind.** Is it factual or is it driven by temporarily tumultuous emotions and old hurts? Ego loves tension and wisdom loves peace.

Reflection Questions

- How does attachment make your life difficult?
- What is your relationship with change?
- What are you working on letting go?
- How have your preferences changed from five years ago?
- Are you rushing through life? How can you slow down and be more present?

chapter 5

What Love Is and What It Isn't

While we often think of love in relation to the intimate feelings between two people that hold together a partnership, there is also the love we have for family and friends, the love we hold for ideas and experiences, and the love we have for ourselves. In all instances, love is something precious, central, and it carries a cohesive quality that brings a sense of unity and harmony within individuals and in the bonds they form with others and the world. To better understand, let's take a closer look at each major application of love.

THE LOVE WITHIN

The love that exists within you demarcates the health of the relationship you have with yourself. How much we understand the depth of our emotional history, the power we have to not run away from our heavier emotions, the courage we have to accept all that we encounter when we turn our attention inward, and the determination we have to evolve into greater versions of ourselves are signifiers of the amount of self-love that we carry within us.

Self-love, meaning the energy you use to care for, heal, and free yourself, is an essential building block that helps you have a peaceful mind and an open heart that is ready for connections with others.

The application of self-love has three components:

1. **Radical honesty with yourself.** This is a continuous process where you make sure that there are no longer any lies between you and yourself. You check in with yourself regularly to confirm there aren't parts of your emotional history that you are hiding from and that you are moving forward in your daily life without intentionally deluding yourself. You embrace truth because you know it will help you evolve even if it is at first difficult to face.

2. **Positive habit building.** This is a deep process built on radical honesty and self-acceptance where you are real with yourself about what harmful habits you need to stop feeding, and you turn your energy to focus on cultivating the characteristics and healthy patterns that you require to live a great life. This is where your self-love truly shines; you do the hard and consistent work that helps you take yourself to the next level. Remember not

to do everything at once; solidifying a few positive habits before adding more can make the journey more sustainable.

3. **Self-acceptance.** Self-love is not just about personal transformation; it is also about deeply embracing who you are at this moment and where you are in your journey. Self-acceptance helps you develop peace with your emotional history so that you can face your past, understand the hardships, and feel motivated to learn from them so that trauma does not need to be repeated or passed down. Acceptance also helps you appreciate your innate imperfection so that you are not harsh with yourself when you inevitably make mistakes.

A lot of the struggles we face can be attributed to a lack of self-love. Self-love impacts how we see our value and self-worth and how deeply we are able to connect with ourselves and other people—literally every facet of life is impacted by our self-love because without it we are out of balance. Self-love creates the inner harmony needed to reach our full capacity.

Self-love is not only a practical set of actions, but also an undeniable measurement that can help gauge the depth of your current and future relationships. Self-love makes having a beautiful life much more possible.

People who double down on kindness, even when life has been rough, bring a special magic into the world.

A hard past has taught them to be cautious and intentional without completely closing their heart.

They treat people gently because they know that many are struggling in silence.

THE LOVE OF FAMILY AND FRIENDSHIP

On a similar level, love is often a way that we describe our connection with our parents, our family, and some of our closest friends. There is power and care in these links that form the web of your life.

When it comes to people and beings we care about, love is a powerful feeling that fills us with warmth, joy, and care.

These essential connections that form our closest circles are not only deeply nourishing but they are comprised of the people that help us mold our place in the world. Human beings are innately communal, we not only thrive together but we understand ourselves in reference to other people. We are not only individuals, but we are also children, siblings, parents, friends, etc. The people we cherish help form our identities and how we see ourselves in daily life. We are relational beings, we evolved to exist in groups because we rely on one another not just for physical needs but for emotional connection. It has been clearly studied how loneliness negatively affects physical health and how important these deep connections are to our well-being. Being deeply seen and heard by another being is an important and validating experience.

It is not uncommon to have difficulty and tension within families and friendships over time, just as can happen in partnerships. One of the major areas of tension within families happens when parents hold very rigid and defined expectations for their children that they either can't or don't want to follow through with. We want those around us to be happy, but at times we are too specific about how we want this happiness to look. Our own trauma often drives us to want to control others. We have trouble loving others as they are, rather than as we want them to be, and we may withhold our love and approval if they don't meet our expectations. This type of love is conditional rather than unconditional. I believe we should live our lives first and foremost for ourselves and follow the path we feel is right while also doing our best to skillfully and gently handle these core relationships in our lives.

Another common issue is when people feel their parents did not show up for them in the way they needed to feel loved and supported growing up. We can't change the past, but as adults we can now try to find the resources and communities we need to fill those gaps, and we can work to cultivate compassion for our parents, who are imperfect beings. Many parents did not intentionally try to hurt their children; sometimes resources were limited or they were trying their best or doing what they thought was right, just as we are.

Life innately has ups and downs, which come with inevitable hardships, but we are fortunate to have people in our lives who we can lean on during turbulent moments. They not only help us, but these are the people who we stand with and support when they too are going through struggles. These bonds with friends and family create situations where the purest form of love, selfless giving, can be enacted. Some of us have experienced serious trauma from family members, but even in the case of chosen family, i.e., dear friends, when these people go through a hardship we are there for them and selflessly give them support. The beautiful part is that these relationships carry the type of love that is reciprocated; you are there for them because you love them, but they are also on standby, ready to support you when you need it. The joy we experience is multiplied greatly when shared with those we love, and hardship is eased when spread over our network of support.

THE LOVE OF WISDOM

Love can also be understood as the fruit of wisdom. It is possible to elevate your love to a supreme level where you view yourself and all beings with the eyes of compassion. To be able to see people and the world through the lens of love is an elevated mental state that requires intentional cultivation.

It is a long road to free yourself of hate and division so that your mind can think of all beings, even the difficult ones who have caused harm, in a compassionate manner, but it is possible to get there. Honestly, that is the apex of personal development and where this journey leads. Having compassion for all beings does not mean you condone harmful actions. One of the beautiful parts of healing your mind and heart is that as much as you heal, your love and peace increase in equal measure; every step yields beautiful results that affect your life positively here and now. And the further you take it, the more you gain.

Love is the primary domain of a mind that has freed itself from suffering. It is the home of sages who have witnessed ultimate truth. In this sense, love and freedom are synonymous. This apex of love is only possible when the mind has risen above the attachments of ego and finally understood that true peace is found in letting go.

LOVE AS A TOOL TO EXPRESS WHAT'S IMPORTANT

To a simpler degree, the word *love* is often used to describe the things and activities that we feel really strongly about. So that when we speak about them there is no confusion that this is something that truly means a lot to us. We often use the word *love* to describe activities that are central to the identity that we have formed. Or to describe aspects of culture like movies or music that have moved us deeply or helped us understand parts of our own story.

In this sense *love* is used as a word that aggregates all the things that we find special; it brings anything that helps support our identity closer to us so that when we are engaging with another person, they have a clear sense of who we are and what we care about. What you love defines you and it helps others get a sneak peek into who you really are.

THE LOVE OF PARTNERSHIP

Before all these other ways we love, the image most of us think of is the love between partners. It is evident in the way they want to be around each other, how they build a new life as a couple, the way they care for each other, and how they see themselves as a team that takes on life and all of its ups and downs. It is an elevated connection that can sometimes last the length of a lifetime. Even if it does not last a lifetime, it is undeniably powerful. It is a bond that is simultaneously intimate, nourishing, and challenging.

Our lives are defined by relationships and romantic connections that end up being some of the most valuable and memorable pieces of our tapestry. We invest a great deal of energy and attention into them and they often lead to the creation of new families, new memories, and new love. It is deeply healing to be seen and loved by another. It nourishes us in a way no other connection does. And so despite the risks and the vulnerability required, we jump in and hope for the best knowing that we can do our best but that not everything is in our control.

WHAT LOVE ISN'T

The greatest enemy of love is attachment. Why? Because it tries to disguise itself as love. There is a similarity between closeness and clinging that easily confuses the mind. A well-fed connection between two people can create a nurturing feeling of closeness while a fear of loss or craving to control creates the type of clinging that tries to grasp another person with tension. Closeness can foster a relationship, while clinging can stifle a relationship and drain it of love.

A combative relationship with nature, one that does not adhere to its primary law of change, will not only create inner struggle, but it will also push people away. Attachment is essentially a refusal to come to terms with change; it's an attempt to keep things the same or under your power. Attachment will most often manifest as an attempt to control. In a relationship, this seeking for control can turn into harmful behaviors like manipulation, selfishness, and a refusal to evolve or allow others to evolve.

In Kahlil Gibran's famous piece "On Marriage," he wrote:

> But let there be spaces in your togetherness. . . .
> Love one another, but make not a bond of love:
> Let it rather be a moving sea between the shores of your souls.
> Fill each other's cup but drink not from one cup.
> Give one another of your bread but eat not from the same loaf.
> Sing and dance together and be joyous, but let each one of you be alone,

Even as the strings of a lute are alone though they quiver
with the same music.

. . . .

And stand together yet not too near together:
For the pillars of the temple stand apart,
And the oak tree and the cypress grow not in each other's
shadow.

Attachment is at the root of behaviors that lead to relationships breaking. Love is meant to be grounded in freedom. Attachment is an opposing force to freedom; it tries to keep things the same, while freedom understands that change is ultimately good.

Attachment will create images in your mind of what you crave the most and it will direct your energy into creating and maintaining them in the external world. Commonly this looks like taking the image of the person you are attracted to and letting that image morph and inflate in your mind. We can end up "falling in love" with the idea we have of someone and whenever the reality of that person deviates from the image we have of them in our mind, we fear the dissonance and fight against it.

Attachment will ask our loved ones to stay the same, but this is impossible when the river of existence constantly flows forward. Human beings are changing, whether they are aware of it or not. Those of us who seek better lives will intentionally embrace change and use it to our advantage so that we can evolve in ways that generate stability, joy, and fulfillment. Even those who do not actively seek to change will slowly morph in their preferences, thought patterns, and interests over time.

Attachment will make it so that your partner changing feels scary, because the person you fell for will slowly alter into someone new. You may even fear that as they change, they will no longer be interested in maintaining a relationship with you.

Asking a person to stay still, to not grow, to remain as the image you cling to in your mind is unfair to them, unrealistic, and this is an ask that is far from love.

Manipulation arises from a deep craving to control, which ultimately stems from attachment. At the root of manipulation is insecurity and fear.

Selfishness is the antithesis of love. At its highest levels, especially when the mind has a lot of cultivated wisdom, a person will have a great capacity to give. Giving is one of the ultimate ways that love is demonstrated. Being self-centered or egocentric can stop love in its tracks because love is only true when it nourishes both people. If the relationship becomes solely about fulfilling the needs and wants of one individual, the other will feel oppressed and hurt.

One of the biggest misunderstandings of love is thinking that the dramatic parts of a relationship are love itself. Drama can feel exciting and enlivening, but is much closer to entertainment and conflict than love. We think this way because we do not see how attachments, the way we crave for things to exist and our attempts to control and mold reality, impact and even dilute the love we have for each other. Attachment is the thing causing hurt, pain, discord, and the rough emotions and mental states that cause strain in our lives. Love itself is an energy that flows with powerful stability and harmony; it is a force that is not selfish or controlling, it is open and profoundly giving. Love is a state of sublime letting go while attachment is the grip of control. *Confusing love with attachment has dire consequences.*

As the mind becomes less conditioned by the past it holds, it becomes easier to see the difference between attachment and love. As your self-awareness develops it becomes clear that love carries a feeling of ease and attachment has a feeling of tension.

We all come into relationships with attachments because 99.99 percent of us are not fully liberated beings who have eradicated the suffering that comes from craving and attachment. A blend of attachment and love is the normal state of our minds, a mixture of roughness and lightness, and we bring all of this into our relationships with our partners and they bring a similar mixture to us. Our beings come together but so do our accumulated traumas, trigger points, and everything else that can create friction between two people. It is sometimes hard for us to see the difference between attachment and love because the drama that comes with relationships is seen as normal and pervasive. But this does not mean that we can't try harder. If we really love the one we are with and if we really love ourselves, we have no other choice but to accept the challenge of growth and do our best to overcome the attachments that make our minds tense and rigid. If there is intentional development of self-awareness, over time it will become easier to see ourselves and examine where our true motivations are coming from. Am I speaking and acting from a place of attachment or a place of love?

Reflection Questions

- How do you define love?
- When have you felt most loved?
- How does someone have to show up for you to feel loved?
- What did you learn from the times when people have failed to love you well?
- Do you feel like your heart is open and ready for connection? How could you open it more?

chapter 6

Love Is Commitment and Understanding

We often see the world in terms of what we want instead of what we can give. Goals and desires that are wrapped in tension lose their sense of balance and devolve into attachments where we make our "happiness" dependent on their outcome. In this sense, we think we are striving for our own happiness, but what we are actually doing is striving for the fleeting pleasure that we feel when we get to control an outcome.

Happiness and pleasure are not the same thing. Happiness comes from a deep sense of inner balance and peace; it is easy to access when your self-love and selflessness are at equal levels. The highest levels of happiness are possible when you allow the truth that everything is changing and will continue to change to inspire you to arrive at the present moment with greater presence. The intentional act of presence, where you are focusing your attention on the wonder of the moment and you are quietly reminding yourself that the moment in front of you is unique and can never be exactly duplicated ever again, makes you cherish the people in your life at a much deeper and genuine level.

Attachment makes things exceedingly difficult in relationships because a healthy partnership requires the sharing of power so that you both feel like equal designers of the life you are crafting together. Preferences and goals are required to design your life. But the mental wiring of attachment often takes these too far—it becomes emboldened and makes desire and craving its primary focus. This builds tension around a certain outcome and creates a limitation on the mind where, as your attachment to a particular outcome increases, your own perspective grows proportionately and you begin to struggle to see the perspectives of others.

Desire in a relationship is healthy to a certain extent. There is nothing wrong with desiring your partner to treat you well or for there to be good communication between the two of you or any of the other qualities that make a relationship harmonious and vibrant. The issue arises when you want everything all at once and in a constant state of perfection. Even people who have done great work on themselves will not be able to show up as the best version of themselves every hour of every single day. Human beings go through natural ups and downs that make it hard to always get things right. We should have a goal to have a healthy and beautiful relationship, and at the same time we should make sure that this goal doesn't convert into getting attached to having a perfect relationship.

VOLUNTARY COMMITMENTS

If desire to have certain things in a relationship is okay but attachment takes things too far, where is the middle ground? Our best option is to focus on commitments. The dangerous thing about attachments is that they can bring out the worst in a person; attachments can morph into controlling behaviors that squeeze the freedom out of a relationship. Commitments, on the other hand, are a combination of honesty and empowerment. Commitments support each person voluntarily offering what they can bring to the partnership. Commitments work when you both let each other know how you would like your relationship to work and once you hear each other's wants you can both reflect and ask yourself, "Is what my partner wants something that I want to willingly do for them and for us?" In relationships that are based on commitments there is no coercion. You do not feel pressured to do things; instead you have information about what your partner desires and out of your own will and love you can decide to meet those desires.

Designing your relationship around commitments makes it so you are both consistently in your power. There is never an underlying feeling that you are obligated to do something, but what you do have is clarity. When you understand clearly how you can support your partner's happiness, you can take it upon yourself to act in ways that are uplifting to you and your partner. What makes commitment work is that there is great joy in seeing your partner happy, seeing them smile and have comfort and security. When the person you love is happy, that happiness will easily bring out the happiness that is inside of you. Sympathetic joy is what makes commitments worthwhile.

Five green flags that
get overlooked:

Kind eyes
Open heart
Good energy
Caring actions
Honest speech

YOU NEED TWO THINGS TO MAKE A RELATIONSHIP BASED ON COMMITMENTS WORK: HONESTY AND RECIPROCITY

Your honesty directly nourishes your vulnerability, which opens up the possibility for greater connection.

Honesty is necessary from both partners. Only through honesty does communication become worthwhile and meaningful. You can talk all day but if you keep avoiding the truth, you are not really communicating. Honesty is the quality that is feeding and making the connection between the two of you deeper and stronger. Saying that honesty can make or break a relationship is not an understatement. If you really love someone, you have to step closer to them with the truth.

You both need to be honest about how you would like your happiness to be supported but you also need to be honest about what is within your capacity to do. If something your partner is asking for feels wrong or is simply not possible, you need to speak up and say so. You are not obligated to fulfill every single one of your partner's desires. The magic of a relationship happens when you are aware of all their desires, and you find the ones that feel doable for you to fulfill. Not in the sense that it is a duty to fulfill them but because it genuinely feels exciting and good for you to do so.

This is why the voluntary commitment approach adds to the harmony of a relationship, because you both are checking in with each other and then yourselves about what is a good idea to act on. Usually what your partner wants and what you want to give are not too far apart; it just requires a bit of honest clarification for things to align more smoothly. A calm and honest conversation can go a long way when it comes to giving you both the understanding you need to be successful in supporting the health and happiness of your relationship.

The same way that honesty needs to work both ways, it must be clear that you are both putting effort into taking care of each other. It takes two people to create a healthy relationship, both doing their best to give love and receive love. One-sided relationships where one partner is doing more of the emotional heavy lifting, doing more of the care work, always being the one who is calm while the other is not, can be quite draining and unsustainable in the long run.

One of the reasons two human beings come together in a relationship is because life is hard. We not only come together because the bond of love is strong, but there is also the added benefit that partnership divides the workload and you have two people doing the problem-solving instead of one. Having someone to bounce ideas off or think things through with is incredibly valuable. If too much of the emotional and physical work of a relationship falls onto one person, the feeling of not being appreciated or the feeling of not having someone care for you properly will start to grow and become a hindrance between the two of you. It's not that you have to split each task fifty-fifty; you each have your strengths. The important thing is you are both contributing and appreciating your partner's efforts. Understanding how to care for each other properly is a long-term goal, but what matters is that the effort is apparent, and that active care is improving.

Making sure that the commitments you make to each other are not lopsided and that you both are taking the love you feel for the other and turning it into a set of actions that feeds the relationship is important. The same way you have to care for yourselves as individuals, you also have to care for the relationship by actively supporting each other's happiness.

ESTABLISH UNDERSTANDING AS YOUR GOAL

When you understand what your ideal relationship looks like, you need to also be aware of what you will need to get there. Just as it is important to establish a relationship that is constructed out of voluntary commitments, it is also important to know that when any friction arises, your goal is not to win, but to understand.

> If we can really understand the problem, the answer will come out of it; because the answer is in the problem, it is not separate from the problem.
>
> *—Jiddu Krishnamurti*

Partners will often miss the opportunity to understand each other because they are too focused on the tension in their minds. It is easy to quickly become attached to feeding the tension in your mind, which makes you pay less attention to what your partner is saying and more attention to how you want to respond so that you can prove you are correct.

Because our minds have a reactive tendency that is often lightning fast, when we feel sad or threatened we will jump into defensive behaviors. Initially we feel like this will make us safe, but when we do this we unconsciously act like our partner is our enemy. This slows down our ability to understand because we are so focused on winning the debate. In reality, there is no debate, even when real mistakes have been made or harm is done, and the better approach is to understand where this behavior is coming from. Understanding has the power to rectify and it has the power to defuse the tension of an argument. When you are able to see things from your partner's perspective and they can simultaneously see things from your perspective, it becomes easier to see the chain of events and how you got to the argument in the first place. It is easier to accept an apology when you can see the root of these emotions and how they fed into the mistakes that were made or the disagreement that arose.

If the goal is to understand each other, and that understanding will be able to defuse the situation, how do we get there?

Trying to apply anything during an argument can feel tremendously difficult, but you must start somewhere. The key thing to establish is to do your best to deliver your truth without getting overheated. Speaking for yourself and using "I" statements are always helpful. Calm communication, even during an argument, can make both of you feel safer so you can let down your defenses and focus on understanding each other, as opposed to feeling like you are in survival mode. Calm communication is not about faking anything; it is simply applying the reasoning that speaking to each other in a respectful manner will help you more efficiently arrive at an understanding that helps you close the chapter on the argument. It also maintains the respect and love you have for each other even in these difficult moments.

Selfless listening is a skill that we all need to intentionally cultivate. It is so easy to get stuck only thinking about our own thoughts and emotions in the midst of an argument. To be able to end the argument in a way where nothing is buried and both people feel genuinely better, each person needs to practice selfless listening so that both stories are clearly understood. Intention can help us focus our energy into simply listening without adding anything on to what we are hearing. Selfless listening is an intentional practice of objectivity—you are taking in the other person's perspective as data that helps you see a picture that is bigger than the narrative your mind wants to cling to. This is especially difficult when you feel wronged, but even in these cases it is worthwhile to hear why your partner did what they did.

Another aspect that helps with understanding is the power of compassion. Once you settle into calm communication and start listening selflessly, do your best to put yourself in your partner's shoes, see things from their perspective so that you can get a better feel for why their actions lined up the way they did. Compassion is the medicine that helps us break out of our confined perspectives.

Seeking to understand each other is doubling down on the great truth that no one is your enemy. Arguments can get so heated that they feel like combat without the physical violence, and in these moments there is the striving for victory where one person wins and the other loses. In these cases, there is a great potential for resentment from both individuals. Seeking to understand not only creates a safer environment for each partner's emotions, but it also makes this moment of tension something that can be quite productive and even help you become closer as a couple.

There is a beautiful level that relationships can enter, where enough emotional maturity is established so that both of you feel safe enough to be authentic and honest. You have each spent enough time and energy establishing the architecture of your emotional home and now you get to enjoy the feeling of security and active care that bonds the two of you. Not only are you two deeply in sync, but you are intentional about treating each other with kindness and curiosity. Life continues its natural ups and downs, challenges come and go, hard moments give you their lessons, but even among it all you two remain assured in your support and care for each other and maintain the goal of elevating the love that flows between you.

Even if this chapter of your lives is harmonious, there is never any expectation of perfection. There are still disagreements between you and things you each will occasionally have to apologize for, but conflict is now held in a different container. Even when you argue you can both still feel that you love the other deeply. There is no malice in your words but instead you are more interested in understanding each other and coming to a resolution that feels good to the both of you. Nothing is flawless, tension and irritation still arise, but happiness has never been more abundant. The inner work that you both put energy into is the key that opens the door to this new era.

Understanding is love's other name. If you don't understand, you can't love.

—Thich Nhat Hanh

PREVENTIVE COMMUNICATION

Preventive communication is designed to help curb unnecessary projections or the buildup of false narratives that cause arguments. Tension will just keep looking for more tension; it is a fire that is constantly looking for kindling to keep expanding. By arriving with honesty and early communication with yourself and your partner, you have a much better chance of removing the kindling that keeps the fire of tension going. In many instances, naming how I felt out loud to Sara actually helped the tension that I was feeling burn itself out faster than if I had just continued keeping it to myself.

We stumbled into preventive communication after years of not fully understanding how our moods greatly impacted our ability to be logical. We would fall into small and sometimes big arguments without realizing that we weren't actually mad at each other, we were just trying to expand the inner tension that we were already feeling in our minds.

Emotions have this uncanny need to expand. Whether they are lighter emotions like happiness and joy or heavier ones like anger and hate, we are often trying to get other people to feel just like we do. If there is lightness in the mind, we like to share it with others. If there is heaviness in the mind, we like for that heaviness to spread so that others can commiserate with us. It feels validating to influence others to feel the same way we do; it is unifying. We share the lighter emotions with our positivity, our infectious smiling, or by outright telling others why we feel the way we do. For heavier emotions we will sometimes tell someone close to us why we are upset so they can join us in the feeling, we will spread negativity with our attitude, or we will rehash old arguments in our mind so that we can be mad at whomever is in proximity to us. Even though we may not be directly sharing the reasons for our low mood, our energy will be full of tension and irritation, which will be clearly palpable to those around us and will often impact their moods, pulling them down.

The last one is something that happens often in relationships; when someone's mood is low, it is easy to see things through a very negative lens. Moods like to feed themselves, so a heavy mood will look for more stories to keep its own fire burning. It will not matter much if the stories are true, based on partial information, or from a very long time ago; the mind will continue generating narratives that keep the tension going. This is a constant challenge in relationships because moods cannot remain flawlessly consistent or positive. They will ebb and flow. But the challenge we encounter is making sure that the lows we experience do not snowball into a delusion that makes us start an argument where there need not be one.

Granted there will be plenty of times when arguments happen for a clear reason. There is no relationship where you are never upset with each other. Arguments are not actually a bad thing—if held with care, honesty, calmness, and vulnerability, they can become a way for the two of you to reach a new level of understanding that helps you love each other better. Arguments can become stepping stones that help advance the relationship. Arguments can also be the force needed to break down a wall that was keeping the two of you away from each other.

But there are more times when we get upset with each other because we are unaware of how we feel inside and how that is driving our thoughts and reasoning to be more turbulent than normal.

During the first few weeks of the pandemic, Sara and I, like the rest of the world, were cooped up inside; for us it was in our little apartment in NYC. We were afraid and worried about what was going on in the world. We were also happy to be spending more time together. At the time I was working from home, writing my second book, *Clarity & Connection*, and Sara was commuting daily to her job as a scientist. Our newfound proximity to each other was quickly revealing. We got to see how much we had grown and how meditation was helping us be calmer and more supportive of each other, but we also started noticing that we still had a lot to work on. Being home together all of the time showed us that we were prone to occasional flare-ups of arguing.

Fortunately, since we were both building self-awareness through meditation, we started realizing that some of the arguments really needed our attention while others seemed built on insubstantial reasons. We started noticing that if we did not feel good one day, the mind would try to not only feed that down feeling, but it liked to project that inner tension onto whoever was nearby. Since we were only near each other, we had to build a system for ourselves so we could clearly see where we each were in our emotional spectrum.

We started intentionally telling each other how we were feeling a few times a day. The most important one was right after we woke up in the morning. Sometimes while still in bed, we would let each other know: I feel great, I'm feeling tired, my mood feels off and stormy, I'm feeling down, etc. We didn't need to justify our mood with a reason we were feeling that way, just the raw emotion was enough. We would do our best to describe how our minds felt in that moment and we found that this quick moment of communication generally set us up to have a successful day together.

We would often have a second emotional temperature check in the middle of the afternoon. After delving into work and facing whatever we had to individually accomplish that day, there was bound to be some impact on how we were feeling. These moments of checking in helped us get the information we needed to support each other well.

If there was a big shift in our emotions at any point in the day, especially one that was unexpected or triggered by something, we would make it known to each other. Having at least two quick and informal check-ins a day and another anytime we felt any big movements in our emotional spectrums helped bring the harmony of our relationship to a level that felt brand-new for us. We were accustomed to having consistent weekly squabbles but a lot of the little ones fell away because we now knew that when one of us was down, offering kindness and asking, "How can I support you in this moment?" helped remove any of the tension that the mind was working on projecting. Having clear information that does not disguise anything really helps address and defuse tension head-on.

One important thing to know about preventive communication is that it is a mixture of asking each other "How do you feel?" and simply volunteering the information without being asked. The informality of preventive communication needs to be embedded in the culture of your relationship for it to be successful. You do not need to sit down and have formal check-ins the way you would during a serious discussion, this is more about getting yourselves accustomed with the truth of the moment and sharing that truth with your partner. You have to be ready to be honest with yourself and not pretend like you feel better than you actually do. For preventive communication to work, you need to cultivate radical honesty with yourself and have an open channel of vulnerability with your partner. This requires deep self-awareness and the courage and strength to embrace the feeling that is currently passing through you. Preventive communication is like a quick moment of compassion.

At first it felt difficult to admit we weren't feeling good, sometimes it even felt like admitting defeat, but as soon as the words were out it felt like a huge weight off our shoulders. Over time this practice has become more natural and spontaneous. If one of us is feeling down or off we try to let the other one know as soon as possible to make the other aware and give them an opportunity to support us if they are able to at the time. At the least it's a heads-up to not take any tension or irritation too personally and for the person who feels down it is a reminder to try to speak gently to their partner.

One of the big understandings that is reinforced through preventive communication is that as you are actively and repeatedly naming the different emotional states that you are experiencing, you are seeing for yourself how quickly emotions change. When we are quiet about how we feel or when we intentionally avoid bringing our awareness to how we feel, it becomes easier to fall into the delusion that a strong emotion will last forever, or at least longer than it actually does. In one day you can feel so many things. Through this informative communication style, you see for yourself how much you change, and it helps you develop a healthy sense of detachment toward the temporary emotion you are feeling. You directly allow yourself to feel whatever is real for you in that moment, but you also embrace that feeling with the understanding that it is an exceedingly temporary and fleeting experience, and in time this heaviness ends. Not only that but in naming the emotion you take a lot of the power away from it and you regain your agency. Trying to ignore or deny the way you are feeling, even just to yourself, can inadvertently give the feeling more power. Despite what temporary emotion is present, you still have the power to act as you wish rather than be overpowered by it.

This understanding began affecting Sara and me so much that we casually started changing our language from saying "I am feeling sad right now" to "It feels like sadness is moving through me right now" or "Wow, I feel this heaviness moving through." The acknowledgment and understanding started making our language more accurately represent what was happening. It shows that "I" is never just one thing or emotion, that who you are exists in an ever-changing spectrum. There is something about correctly assessing the impermanence of any emotion in the language that we use that feels truly empowering. Any storm is just that, a storm, and no storm in the history of the world has ever lasted forever.

Eight Lessons from Eight Years of Marriage

Sara and I recently celebrated eight years of marriage. It has been a beautiful and challenging journey to build harmony into our relationship, especially in the beginning before we started meditating. We are not perfect and there are still ups and downs, but undeniably there is more love and care between us than ever before. The following are eight of the main lessons I have learned from our relationship:

1. **Connection alone is not enough.** Sara and I have always had a strong connection, one that feels undeniable and unavoidable, but we struggled to take care of ourselves and each other before we got married. We had very little emotional maturity between the two of us so we were constantly placing unnecessary blame on each other, and we would struggle to apologize and move forward from arguments. Connection can hold you together for only so long; eventually you need to support it with both people doing their own internal work. When both of you develop inner peace and self-awareness, it will flow outward and support your relationship.

2. **Projections cause friction.** A lack of self-awareness was a major struggle for both of us in the beginning. We could not see how we were constantly projecting our emotions onto each other, thus creating misunderstanding. If you are constantly projecting, it means you primarily see just your own point of view and struggle to see the perspective of others. Projections not only create disharmony, but they make each person feel not fully seen by the other. Developing awareness of your own

emotions, seeing them change within you and noticing how they impact your own perspective and your choice of words is a gift that you give yourself and your partner. Self-awareness can help you slow down so you can ask yourself, "Is this really how I feel, or am I just projecting?"

3. **Emotional temperature check-ins are needed.** The simple truth is that even when you have been together for many years, you will not be able to read each other's minds. The next best thing is checking in with each other a few times a day about where your emotions are. Letting each other know how your moods are shifting not only helps your communication, but it functions as a preventive measure so that you don't project your emotions onto each other. If you move through the day without acknowledging how you feel, it can be easy to unconsciously blame your partner for down moments that may have nothing to do with them. Being honest and vocal about how you feel brings more clarity to each of your interactions and allows you two to support each other better.

4. **You need to individually understand your emotional history and behavioral patterns.** Personal inner work is the great game changer in a relationship—it has the

power to create a new era of understanding and skillful behavior that will help you have a deeper and more joyful union. If you do not acknowledge the way your past has shaped you, you will continue repeating the same defensive and survivalist reactions you used back then. If your past remains unconscious, it will seep into your relationship in ways that block you and your partner from having the best union possible. Only after you see yourself clearly can you work toward developing new habit patterns that are more conducive to supporting your own happiness and your partner's.

5. **Finding and using a healing practice is the real work.** Becoming aware of your emotional history is one thing, changing it is another. Once you see your knots, you then have to untangle them. The best way to do that is by picking up an established practice that is already helping many people. There is no need for you to reinvent the wheel. You just need to find something that meets you where you are, something that aligns with your intuition and helps you take tangible steps forward. For Sara and me, it was Vipassana meditation, but there are many different forms of meditation out there that can bring good results, or different forms of therapy and many other practices that can help. You also should realize that you and your partner may need different healing tools and that is okay, what matters is that the work is actually hap-

pening and that you are both creating space for changed behavior.

6. **Let each other evolve.** Who you both were on the first day you met each other is worlds apart from who you are now. Whether intentionally or unintentionally, your likes, dislikes, strengths, and general preferences will change over time. This is not something that you should resist; it is an incentive to remain curious about each other as time moves forward. There is always more you can learn about each other and the ways you like to receive support will also morph over time. Your individual evolution will spur on the evolution of your relationship. What the two of you find funny, how you like to enjoy rest, what you like to learn together, the places you like to visit, how you view the world—all of these will have slight or great transformations over time.

7. **You are more than partners; you are also best friends and roommates.** Expanding your idea of the roles you play in each other's lives can be beneficial. Sara is not only the love of my life, she is also my best friend. We enjoy telling each other everything and we face the world as a team. Sharing our living space together makes us roommates by default, and a big part of our relationship is mutually creating a space that feels like home to the both of us. Your partner is not only the person who you

share many laughs with, they are also the primary person you plan and strategize with so that you can properly face any challenges that arise. Seeing each other as playing a multifaceted role is not about codependency, it is simply admitting the fact that any relationship between two people is versatile.

8. **The truth brings you closer together.** Lies always create distance. If you really want to feel like a team and elevate your connection, you have to be honest with each other. Honesty is sometimes difficult to give but doing so in a compassionate manner helps. Receiving honesty is also difficult, but it is better than living in a house of lies. Once you open the door to honesty, there may still be much to resolve and talk over, but in time, if that door stays open, you both will feel a new level of confidence in your relationship. You will both know that you are committed to each other and that your communication is strengthening. There is a sense of freedom and lightness that you will each feel when you know that the truth is welcome in your relationship.

Reflection Questions

- How does it feel when you recognize that someone is genuinely understanding you?
- What commitments have you made to another person that you feel great about?
- Are you someone who shies away from commitment out of fear of getting hurt? How are you working on unbinding this pattern?
- Have you taken the time to go deep and connect with your partner lately?
- What are some understandings about yourself or your relationship you'd like to communicate with your partner this week?
- Do you notice the way your emotions change during the day? Are you open to sharing these changes with your partner?

chapter 7

The Art of Arguing

Without understanding, love is an impossible thing.

—Thich Nhat Hanh

When you understand that relationships are not just a space of safety and nourishment, but they are also a space that fuels your evolution, you will no longer be surprised when moments of struggle arise between you and the one you love.

When a fight arises it does not necessarily mean that the two of you are not right for each other. The survivalist mind will see an argument as dangerous and it will want to make excuses as to why it needs to convince you to run. This is why pausing before you speak to gather yourself and assess how you want to show up in an argument is vital. This will help you shift from a survivalist mindset into an intentional one that seeks to repair as opposed to control.

When you start seeing that occasional arguments are actually a natural part of being close to another human being, you will stop treating the challenging moment as a "bad thing" and instead you will see it as an opportunity to understand each other better. As long as both of you care about each other more than about being right, a resolution and end to the argument will eventually come to fruition. Being serious about personal growth and having the ability to see more than just your own perspective will also help as you navigate disagreements.

It is unreasonable to expect that a relationship will have no conflict. Since both of you have egos and because those egos have acquired a lifetime of conditioning, some of which is defensive conditioning built during times of survival or struggle, there are bound to be moments when you have to sit down and seriously discuss the friction that is arising between you. Even so, when you both double down on living as the mature versions of yourselves, you can be intentional about holding your arguments within a loving container.

The following are some key practices that can help facilitate a smoother transition from argument to understanding.

1. **Valid perspectives.** You each have your own perspective on the matter and each perspective deserves to be fully listened to without interruption. The only way the two of you can develop a full view of what happened between you is by bringing your two perspectives to-

gether. The key practice here is patiently taking turns to give each other the space to share before you have an open discussion about how to move forward.

2. **Practice selfless listening.** Your ego will try to get in the way when your partner is sharing their side of things, and the only way to combat this is by intentionally refocusing your attention on their words instead of thinking about how you want to respond to what they are saying. This is a practice of compassion. Let yourself be immersed in their view of things; see it from their angle. This can only work if you both take turns being the selfless listener.

3. **Be honest without being dramatic.** The drive to be correct can make you embellish things. Can you be honest and express yourself without going overboard or being mean? Leaning into an honest demonstration of your perspective will make the conversation move more smoothly and it will bring you closer together. The deepest forms of love require a foundation of honesty and gentleness.

4. **Ask yourself if you can let it go.** Attachment happens quickly when the ego feels threatened—even if the line of reasoning you are getting attached to is illogical and

functioning as a roadblock that stands in the way of your peace. Check in with yourself to see if you are hanging on to heated emotions unnecessarily. Remember the love you have for your partner and the love you have for yourself. Let these lighter emotions guide you to a middle path.

5. **Take responsibility for your part of it.** When we take responsibility for our actions and mistakes it creates a space where others feel more comfortable doing the same. No one person in a partnership should always have to be the bigger person, but when you can accept your part in something, own up to it, and apologize for it, this changes the discussion from one of blame to one of connection.

6. **Remember, your partner is not your enemy.** Don't let your anger make you forget who is in front of you. The person in front of you is not perfect, but they are still the one you love. Make sure to protect yourself, hold them accountable if necessary, but do not be overly confrontational.

7. **The goal is not to win but to understand.** When you realize that love has nothing to do with dominance and everything to do with freedom, it becomes easier to focus

on understanding each other as a way to conclude the argument instead of winning. Understanding is a generative emotion, whereas if you strive to win, that means the other person has to lose, which will naturally lead to the accumulation of resentment. Seeking to understand means you both welcome vulnerability, which will help deepen your connection.

Find a partner who is emotionally aware enough to have a calm and honest conversation when the two of you are experiencing conflict.

Seeking to understand each other instead of winning the argument makes it easier to find a common ground that you both feel good about.

Both of you accept the truth that love is not easy and that being imperfect is natural.

Even during storms, you don't forget your love for each other and how much you value your connection.

FURTHER ON PERSPECTIVE

When you understand that your own perspective is limited and clouded by your past perceptions, you will cling to it less. The mind cannot immediately process multiple perspectives, and therefore a greater amount of the truth, unless you train it to do so. Perception is normally ego centered and focused on your singular point of view as well as being filtered through your past, but most situations, especially those dealing with other people, are created through a myriad of causes. This means that what you see, how you felt, what you think happened, are not the entirety of the picture; there is so much more going on than the story your mind is forging together. A singular moment that people share can be understood in a variety of different ways.

It takes a lot of mental strength and humility to recognize that your perspective does not equate to full truth. Being able to let go of the story in your mind opens you up to the possibility of co-creation, where you build a new and more expansive narrative of the series of events with the person or people it involves—this is especially important for couples. Co-creating the story by listening to each other selflessly will paint a much clearer and more honest picture than if one person is attempting to dominate the narrative and fully avoid all blame.

This does not mean that you have to exactly agree on how everything happened, but it does mean that you have to intentionally take turns stepping out of your own perspective to see how your partner experienced the situation. The simple act of stepping out of your own perspective is a demonstration of your love for your partner. This act is a clear signal that you care about them and respect them as an equal, that they have a fair say over how everything transpired. Neither of you control the narrative because you are building it together.

During a tough conversation, it is important to check in with yourself about the status of your emotions or if the situation has triggered old hurts. If your emotions feel too hot, then surely they can impact your perception and make what happened even cloudier than before. When your emotions feel exceedingly turbulent, it will be hard for you to step outside of your own perspective. Dense emotions contain the energy of clinging, they will stick to whatever is fueling them. This means that heavy emotions will look back on the series of events and they will incline themselves toward seeing the other person as the one who is in the wrong; this helps the emotions stay hot, but it doesn't provide a solution. In these moments, it may be best to tell your partner that your emotions feel so rough that they are making it hard for you to think in a balanced manner and ask to come back to the discussion after you have had some time to cool off. Not everything needs to be addressed immediately, and sometimes it can be really healthy to calm down before discussing an argument.

When I look back at the arguments Sara and I had over the many years we have been together, most of them ended with the both of us apologizing. When we settled down into intentional calmness and started speaking honestly about the series of events, it would become clear that we both did things that actually made the argument more tense. Neither of us was a saint, we both said things we regretted, and in time we would apologize and own up to the mistakes we made. Even when one of us clearly started an argument and had more to apologize for, the other usually accepted the invitation into anger and ended up saying or doing things that just made the situation worse. Realizing how easy it is to add to the problem and that you and your partner are not perfect people will help you have the humility to apologize when it is necessary.

LETTING GO OF THE SMALL THINGS

Human beings are constantly moving through a wide spectrum of emotions and whenever you are going through a heavier mood it becomes much easier to say or do something that you later regret or that your partner finds hurtful. A lot of arguments and moments of tension between couples are triggered by small things. One person doesn't feel great that day so they are more sensitive than usual or someone takes a joke too far, etc. In these cases, you each have a choice: to apologize and forgive or to allow the tension to snowball and let it become something way bigger than it needs to be. A mundane and simple mistake can quite easily get connected to a larger overarching problem that has been a difficult and reoccurring point of contention in your relationship. Usually this is because the emotion of anger or resentment will look for more to feed itself and the easiest thing to do is just to rehash the big problems in your relationship that you two often come back to.

When you make the intentional building of your self-awareness a natural aspect of your daily life, you will begin to notice when you are enlarging a small point of tension and the way your mind will start connecting disparate things to make itself more tense. When you recognize this process beginning in your mind, you should practice letting go. If you honestly assess yourself, you will see that there were many arguments in your life that did not need to happen, moments of tension that became unnecessarily big.

Something like not getting enough sleep one night or being hungry can become the catalyst for big arguments with your partner. We often miss these small connections between our mood and our negative reactions because we so quickly get caught up in the object of our frustration.

Small things can become bigger quite quickly—but do they need to?

One of the most beautiful ways to express your love for another human being is to do your best to see them clearly and not react out of a bad mood or past patterns.

This is possible when you understand that past conditioning and present circumstances will often color your view of what another person is saying and doing. The hurt you carry, the trauma you may have experienced, as well as the inevitable down moments in life, will adjust your perception, usually in a defensive direction. Often when you look at another, you will initially see your own emotions instead of seeing the person as they are. When it comes to love, the past can sometimes be our biggest obstacle in developing a healthy and vibrant connection.

If you want to love another person well, you have no choice but to journey inward and make sure that the love within you is open, inviting, and that it is ready to receive and give nourishment.

The best way to do this is by putting effort into three things:

1. **Spending time examining your emotional history.** This will help you understand yourself more completely. It will show you your strengths and the parts of you that need healing. What is within you will manifest itself in your relationships one way or another, so it will serve you to be aware of your deepest patterns.

2. **Making sure you do not run away from tough emotions in the present moment.** If you can be with

yourself during turbulent moments, this will greatly enhance your patience and your capacity to understand that storms are not everlasting. Letting these heavy moments pass through you without taking control of you will help you eventually feel lighter and give you a great ability to be there for another person when they are struggling.

3. **Intentionally creating a loving relationship between you and yourself.** How you treat yourself can easily become how you treat your partner. Loving another person is greatly shaped by how strong your self-love is. The ways you accept yourself, such as talking to yourself gently in your mind, not forcing yourself to be perfect, and all the other ways you activate your self-love, will end up framing the shape of your relationship.

Making your perception clearer also requires intentional mental training. Teach yourself to observe things without immediately jumping to conclusions, to suspend evaluation and just take in what's happening. It also requires bringing yourself back to the present moment repeatedly so that your mind doesn't immediately swim to the past or the future. The deepest act of love is not a memory or wanting something in the future, it is a selfless action in the present moment.

These skills you develop will come in handy in daily life as you and your partner take turns listening so you can try to see the world through the other's unique perspective. The ability to genuinely listen is compassion in action. When you both intentionally try to listen to each other selflessly and enter into conversations with curiosity, your connection will naturally get stronger and more fulfilling. The pure attention you give each other will bring you closer together.

ASSUMPTIONS AND EXPECTATIONS

Remind yourself often that your partner cannot read your mind. Even after years of being together, they can know your story well, they can understand your triggers and support your goals, but they cannot know the intricate and complex movement of your thoughts. Creating a culture between the two of you where communication comes first can set the foundation for a loving partnership. It also can remove any confusion that may arise from keeping important information to yourself that could help the relationship.

The mind does not like unknowns so it will rapidly try to fill in the blanks. Even when it comes to your relationship, it will be quick to make assumptions. This pattern is so deeply ingrained in the mind that it will jump to making assumptions even when these assumptions are based on scarce and unverifiable pieces of information. Especially if fear is an emotion that your mind runs to often, it will create negative assumptions that have no basis in reality. The mind can make you see threats and challenges where there are none. It can make you question your partner's intentions or even the love they have for you.

Assumptions are treacherous territory; they can create a rift between you and your partner and make you both feel like you can't trust the other. The only way to close this gap between you is with truthful communication and by slowing down when you are the one jumping to conclusions. *Instead of assuming, ask. If you are building unreliable narratives on partial information, ask your partner for the information you need to truly understand them.*

The act of continually making assumptions, especially when they are fear based, can wear down your partner and make them feel like your relationship doesn't have adequate trust. This can especially be the case if a previous partner has hurt or betrayed you—the mind will jump to the conclusion that a new partner may be up to the same antics. But that is not always the case. Don't let assumptions be the reason trust cannot flourish in the home you are building together.

Silent expectations can also create a rift between you and the one you love. Expectations are often unvoiced needs or wants, ways that you would like your partner to support your happiness, but that they may be unaware of. The problem is that they are not properly communicated. Unspoken expectations are like little traps that you unconsciously set for yourself and your partner. You get upset when your silent expectations are not met even though your partner never had the information they needed to see if meeting your need was within their capacity. Remember, silent expectations are a recipe for disappointment and future arguments.

Both assumptions and unspoken expectations are a failure of communication. Their immediate remedy is to have the courage to be more honest with each other and to not let your minds run away and create untrue narratives. Your partner deserves the chance to be the best partner possible, but that requires you giving them a high level of insight into your mind so that they are well informed about how to best support you. A good way to show your love is to clearly tell each other what the other is doing well and what they could do better.

Making them guess what you need will simply create disappointment for both of you.

CALM COMMUNICATION

I am fortunate not only to have great parents, but also to have great in-laws. I am grateful to have a wonderful relationship with my in-laws. They have been welcoming, kind, and incredibly supportive. Sara's parents, Jan and Steve, have taught me a tremendous amount, mostly from the example of how they live their lives and from how they treat each other and those around them. Over the years I have always noticed the way the two of them will have important discussions with each other in a calm manner. Even through the ups and downs, they maintain a clear level of compassion for each other as they solve problems together.

Jan and Steve have been married for forty-eight years and have six kids together. One of the biggest gifts they have given to their family is their inner stability and the strong love they have for each other. The atmosphere that they have cultivated in their home partially stems from an important moment they shared right after they were married. They were in the midst of a discussion, but they were disagreeing with each other very strongly.

As many people do, Steve began to raise his voice as he was expressing himself. Jan looked at him and said: "Stop, wait a second, I want to have a lot of arguments with you. I look forward to many years of disagreeing, but just don't raise your voice to me. Please don't yell. If you raise your voice at me, I can't hear you." This moment completely changed how they talked to each other.

From Steve's perspective, he felt accused of yelling, when he was actually just raising his voice. But he recognized that to Jan it did qualify as yelling, so he stopped. He knew that even though their perceptions of that moment were different, to continue in the same way was not conducive to good communication that could help them overcome the disagreement. Jan clearly expressing her feelings during this moment early in their relationship created an opportunity to pivot. Over time, Steve saw that even without raising his voice, he was able to get his point across.

I am particularly struck by the powerful line, "I want to have a lot of arguments with you" because it fundamentally captures a truth of long-lasting relationships. You are not going to agree all of the time. You are two individuals with your own viewpoints and the turbulence of life will create moments when those viewpoints will come to the surface and sometimes they will not mesh well.

Even so, there should be a standard, a culture developed between you and your partner that encourages placing these disagreements within a conducive container, where the conflict is not an opportunity for ego to grow and dominate, but instead for compassion to come to the surface so you can understand each other at a deeper level. Arguing is normal, disagreeing is common, but love is the way the two of you can lift your heads above the water so that you can find a good path forward.

Jan went on to say that to be able to argue for years they both needed to be able to listen, feel heard, and not feel attacked in the middle of a disagreement. Even though this moment happened decades ago, it has rippled through time and set the standard for productive communication between the two of them. The calm communication they practice is even apparent in the way they speak to their children and grandchildren. Moments of authenticity and having the courage to make your needs clear can end up positively impacting many people down the line.

Find a partner who can clearly remember
that they love you even when you two
are having an argument.

You know the love is real because
even when they are upset they are still curious
to understand things from your perspective.

As you each keep sharing,
you start letting go of the tension
and find a middle ground that
feels good to both of you.

ON BLAME

The ego is incredibly fond of blame. It has the tendency to reject accountability and responsibility. The ego will feel negative emotions and always seek to assign external reasons as to why they are happening, even when it has to bend logic to do so. The ego is a temporary, fear-based mechanism that helps us navigate the material world, but its primary object is survival, and it is continuously hungry for pleasantness.

Part of the difficulty of taking ownership over how you feel is that reclaiming your power comes with discomfort. It is much easier to point the finger at others than to see how much of your misery is self-created. We use the language "my ego took a hit" because this is exactly what it can feel like to accept responsibility for your mistakes. Shame and embarrassment may at first accompany accepting accountability, but this is the more mature and even powerful thing to do, and those initial emotions often fade quickly.

Developing a balanced view on blame requires not going to extremes and realizing that every issue that arises is situational and dependent on the conditions that caused it. The cause will not always be the same.

The key thing to understand is that the reality you are experiencing is being filtered and composed by your mind. Your perception is a dominant aspect of your mind; it will take in the information it is encountering and relate it to past memories. Your perception does not just perceive, it also evaluates. Without even bothering to make sure that what you are perceiving is correct, the mind will give it a positive or negative evaluation. This is an incredibly fast process that can sometimes land us in trouble in our daily lives because we end up too quickly assessing what we encountered. Instead of simply observing, we jump straight into judging. This reactive quality of the mind makes sense when you are struggling for survival, but it can complicate interpersonal situations.

We are not only creating quick judgments, but we are reacting to how those judgments make us feel. This lightning-fast process is happening entirely in our minds. This is one of the hardest truths to accept, because at an ultimate level, our own suffering is happening inside our minds, and it is affected by how we perceive reality. This can feel simultaneously daunting and inspiring because you are the maker of your life, you are directly responsible for creating the reality you are experiencing by the way you are evaluating it. This does not discount the very real fact that others can also cause us harm; it is just highlighting that our mental reaction to external experiences can greatly increase or decrease the suffering we experience.

The past is heavily influencing how we perceive the present, so much so that it is completely intruding on our ability to create new objective observations because it is trying hard to categorize whatever you are encountering through what it has experienced before. Being intentional about freeing yourself from the past, by bringing awareness into this process and taking the time to slow down and suspend judgment, can help you see things in a fresh and genuine way.

The past can be so heavily coded in our minds that we could hear a string of words from someone who has pure intentions and who means no harm and our minds will remember that those exact words were said years ago by someone who hurt us greatly. Immediately our minds will associate the person in front of us with the person who hurt us in the past, and instinctively we may close ourselves off to whatever else the new person is saying.

The combination of relating everything you are presently experiencing with your past and the ego's rejection of taking responsibility creates ample potential for blame, arguments, and moments of tension between partners. Especially when humans naturally like to share their tension with whomever is closest to them. We are beings of proximity, which means that those nearest to us will get the best and the worst of us.

The primary way to stop this lightning-fast process of judgment and rejection of responsibility is by slowing down and challenging yourself to remain as honest as possible. It takes intentional energy to develop a balanced perspective. Slowing down and teaching yourself to refrain from jumping to conclusions or from quickly developing a narrow viewpoint based on past emotions is necessary if you want to take in the present in as objective a manner as possible. *Being objective is difficult for human beings because truth is secondary to survival.* But we can train our minds to understand that there is great benefit to being more balanced in the way we assess situations, especially when it comes to relationships. We need to have a sense of objectivity so we can own up to our mistakes and apologize when it is necessary to do so.

Objectivity itself is a serious challenge and hard to measure, especially when it comes to relational situations. You know you have gotten closer to objectivity when both you and your partner feel heard and understood when resolving the tension between you. If both of you feel that you can see each other more clearly, the heated tension in your minds is lessening, and you are each accepting responsibility for your part of the issue, then you are getting closer to finding a middle path.

Even when someone clearly starts an argument or does something they need to apologize for, the other person usually adds tension to the situation. Granted, there are definitely times when an argument is one person's fault, but we have to ask ourselves honestly, "How many times have I made an argument that I didn't start worse by acting out my agitation and ended up saying something that I later regretted?" Again, saints are rare.

To achieve balance, it is essential to understand that your own perception and reactions are feeding the tension in your mind, which means that you won't always be able to maintain inner harmony when someone is trying their best to upset you. But you can keep trying. *Reclaim your power from the people around you who are trying to invite you to join them in their rough emotions.* At the same time, also realize that this does not excuse mean behavior toward you. Sometimes people will do or say things that are undoubtedly wrong and we should stand up for ourselves and others who are being wronged. Reclaiming our power in this sense is not about suppressing our emotions, it is about managing our blind reactions so they don't become overblown and further cloud our perceptions and actions.

Be mindful of how much blame you are placing on each other. Be mindful of how much the tension in your mind can twist your logic and convince you to argue with someone when it is actually unnecessary. Check in with yourself by asking, "Was this tension in my mind before I even started thinking about them?"

Reflection Questions

- Could you listen better to your partner? Can you challenge yourself to listen more selflessly the next time you argue?
- Are you aware when your ego is trying to defend and protect itself in an argument?
- Are you and your partner able to get to the root of the issue and hold each other compassionately?
- Can you think clearly after someone says something triggering? What do you need to rebalance yourself?
- What are some ways you keep your ego in check during an argument?

chapter 8

The Challenges Relationships Face

BEFRIENDING THE CHALLENGE OF LOVE

Many people want the most beautiful aspects of a relationship: the love, care, joy, and support, but they don't want any of the challenges that come with loving someone with the entirety of their heart. When you watch movies about love, you often see two people meeting, and then they face a single challenge. With some courage, they overcome it and finally fully commit to each other. The quietly misleading part is that we don't see what happens after, and our subconscious conditioning slowly adopts the thinking that "happily ever after" means there won't be further challenges in a loving partnership.

In a real-life relationship, there are constant struggles of all shapes and sizes. For many who are dealing with health issues, family issues, or financial issues, just trying to find time and space to be in a loving relationship can feel especially hard. Family and careers also come with their inevitable ups and downs and can create real stress. I don't have children myself right now so I won't speak to this in detail, but at the very least, children add a whole new dynamic to your relationship that takes a lot of your focus and energy away from each other. I have seen this happen often with family members and close friends. The way you are when you are just with your partner will inevitably change when children come into the picture. Loving and supporting each other becomes even more important in these different stages of your life together. But when done well, a strong relationship can be the thing you lean on when life gets hard.

Even if at the conscious level we admit to ourselves that life and relationships continuously have ups and downs, when a challenge actually appears, we don't like it and we hope it goes away as fast as possible without having to do anything. This makes sense because our survival instinct craves safety and predictability, but the nature of reality is one of continuous and uncontrollable change. Even though disliking hard moments is a default for many of us, life and love will ask us to go beyond our initial patterns if we want to live fulfilling lives.

A lot of people are scared to commit because of the fear that they may be missing out on someone better who they have not yet met, someone who can help them escape their problems and make life easy. Many relationships never even get off the ground because too many people crave "easy."

Some repeatedly choose to not begin a genuine relationship and they opt out of feeding a great connection that is right in front of them because they are too attached to the idea of perfection. The craving for a "perfect" partner rather than a unique individual with strengths and areas they can grow in keeps them on an endless chase.

Others sometimes self-sabotage relationships because they don't feel worthy or good enough and because they have a lot of old hurt to unpack and release. The truth many forget is that it is possible to work on healing yourself while also being in a healthy relationship. Waiting to be perfectly healed before you let yourself love someone is going to an unnecessary extreme. No one enters a relationship as a flawless human being.

These are just a few of the main mental and emotional blocks that prevent compatibility and connection from blossoming into profound relationships.

Befriending the challenge of love is the true task of anyone who wants to cultivate a long-term relationship. Once you let go of the ideas of easy, perfect, and not being good enough, you can ground yourself in reality and realize that the feeling of connection can be the beginning of something truly special. Connection is a magnetic pull that gives two people the signal that it is worth investing energy into each other. Even though you may feel fear in the face of vulnerability and potential heartache with a new person or agitation when an argument arises, these are opportunities for growth and problem-solving or for understanding each other better, instead of openings to run away. The thing you have to remember is that *fear can stop a connection from blossoming.*

A relationship is not an escape, it is a deep form of arrival: one where if you want it to succeed, you will have to face yourself with great honesty and give your partner a high level of presence so you can keep feeding the connection the two of you have. In this case, presence means listening with the intention to understand, attention, energy, compassion, eye contact, thoughtful questions, the curiosity to learn more about the other's perspective, and the readiness to be vulnerable. Giving each other deep presence is what elevates a connection and allows it to unfold into a home you both find nourishing. Presence is needed to make someone feel loved. It takes time for the magic of a relationship to fully activate.

We all have to remind ourselves that connection alone does not create an incredible relationship, but choosing to face fears and challenges together and learning how to care for each other does. There is always a need for a learning period when you really focus on discovering each other so you can begin to love each other well. Consistently running away and choosing to not go all in on someone great removes the possibility of building a beautiful relationship. Of course, you have to make sure the connection is worthwhile, but running at the first sign of difficulty ends the potential for real love.

UNEXPECTED CHALLENGES

My close friends Soren and Cecily are one of the couples I look to for inspiration. The way they listen to each other with deep presence and treat each other with genuine compassion is active care at its finest. You can see the love shine brightly when their eyes connect and you can feel that they have both spent a lot of time working on themselves because of their balanced temperaments. It is a joy to be in their presence and to benefit from their calm and focused attention. Cecily and Soren got together in their middle years, when both already had children from previous marriages as well as successful careers.

Relationships are full of unexpected challenges. About a year and a half after Soren and Cecily started dating, Cecily received the harrowing news from her doctor that she had breast cancer. After receiving this life-changing information, Cecily spent time processing how this would impact her life, her kids, her work, and her relationship.

Over dinner, she told Soren that he did not have to stay with her. She said, "I would understand if this is not a journey you want to be on for your life." Soren quickly and honestly told her that leaving her during this pivotal moment had never crossed his mind. The way he said those words made Cecily believe him right away. She was startled by his immediate devotion because she was still processing deep unlearning around love relationships—up to this conversation it had been hard to fathom that a partnership did not have to be transactional.

That dinner was a big moment of vulnerability for both of them. Soren let Cecily know that he deeply trusted her and that if anything were to ever happen to him in the future regarding his health, he would trust her to make decisions for him. Hearing this had a very dramatic impact on Cecily. Seeing the real depth of their connection made Cecily feel like she was being loved in a way that she had not felt before, more selflessly and completely.

In that dinner, they were both profoundly committing to each other, to continuing to move forward as a couple. Even though the future was full of unknowns and imperfections, they were willing to face it all as a team. They were both intentionally doubling down on their love. Thankfully, today Cecily is doing much better health-wise, and together, she and Soren are continuing to learn and practice unconditional love.

Relationships are a commitment to journey through life

together. There will be moments that happen that will be totally unexpected. Challenges will arise that will deeply test you as individuals and as a couple. Being there for each other to share both the greatest highs and the deepest lows is one of the highest forms of love.

People who care about growing and
developing their emotional intelligence
are quiet heroes.

A hard past hasn't stopped them;
it actually is the source of their inspiration
to treat themselves and other people gently.

Every relationship is incredibly unique, but there are some common denominator challenges that many of us will likely face, such as ego, speed of growth, not growing in exactly the same ways, our partner's triggers, trust, and comparison in the social media age, that deserve a more detailed discussion.

EGO

The ego's main goal is to survive and it will defend itself, sometimes blindly, to achieve this. Relationships are challenging because when two human beings are in proximity to each other, there is the potential for friction to occur. Egos are inherently rough and they struggle to accept responsibility for their mistakes. The ego would rather place blame because seeing the fault in others is easier than accepting responsibility and the need for personal growth. The ego lives in its own perspective; it experiences reality as if it were the center of all things, which makes it really hard for it to see beyond its own perceptions. The ego is also easily tricked by its perception, where it sees its perspective as truth as opposed to a stream of clouded information.

What we feel and what we know is all filtered through the ego, which makes creating a space that welcomes vulnerability and takes responsibility for mistakes a task that requires real effort. The ego is great at passing judgment and it processes situations through its defensive framework because the purpose of the ego is survival. But if you go into a relationship with a mentality that is geared toward survival, then you will quickly look upon your partner as a challenger or, even worse, an enemy. If the ego is always on the lookout for danger and in a defensive mode, it can easily twist the information it is processing and create a narrative where it believes that a threat is there that is in no way real.

Overcoming the limitations of ego is a massive task, not just for your own well-being and peace of mind, but for the sake of creating harmony and nourishing interactions in your relationship. Ego makes communication with yourself and with other people difficult. Teaching yourself to loosen the way you cling to your thoughts, and understanding that thoughts are not facts, they are just perceptions, will help you parse through what is valuable and what isn't.

Your ego also wants to make your relationship just about you, but relationships are not about getting everything you want; they are a mixture of giving and receiving. Truly, they are about building a balance where both people feel seen, understood, and loved. Trying to get everything you want in a relationship creates a situation of dominance, where your attachment to what you crave is stronger than the drive to support your partner's happiness. Focusing your energy on trying to control outcomes squeezes the fun and freedom out of a relationship and instead fills it with tension.

You know the love you feel for your partner is real when you genuinely want to see them happy and you feel comfortable letting them take the reins to lead the relationship in a balanced way. Treating your relationship as something you are co-creating together can make the journey of designing your lives more joyful. Part of feeling accomplished as an individual is finding spaces where you can exercise your power in a healthy way. This is especially important in the safety of your relationship. This can be in something as simple as taking turns deciding what is for dinner, how you will use your weekend, where you will go on vacation, etc. For big decisions, like where you want to live or if you want to have kids, it's very important for both partners to be in agreement. In all decisions, one partner may defer to the other when there is trust and no big inclination on their part, but even in these situations there should be the opportunity to add your two cents and agree. Knowing that the relationship equally belongs to both individuals quietly strengthens the feeling of home.

When both of you are vocal about what you want, it will help you see where you can each let go so that the other can receive. This consistent communication will help you keep your egos from taking charge too often.

SPEED OF GROWTH

When you are in a relationship where both partners embrace their growth, it can still be tricky to accept that people grow at different speeds and sometimes in different directions. Even if the two of you are working on developing similar qualities, it does not mean that you will arrive at victorious points where you see all your efforts paying off at the same time.

The major point of difference here is that you two may have similar aims, but the contents of your mind that you are working on deconditioning are not the same. The load of patterns that you each carry, how many times you have been hurt, the extensiveness of trauma, the ways that you were raised, and all of the conditioning that you acquired in your life will look different for each of you. The contents of your mind are unique to you.

Taking healing seriously does not mean that the healing process will be fast—in fact, it should not be rushed. Especially when the hurt is deep, you will have to let go and repeatedly reframe your mind into more productive ways of thinking and perceiving. The same way that the behavior patterns and habits that you wish to change were created out of repetition, the qualities that you wish to develop also need to be repeated many times over until they finally stick and become a natural part of the new you.

Accept that your partner's inner journey is their own. It may take a significant amount of time for the patterns that they want to undo to fully diminish. There may be times when you both share a goal and you clearly arrive at it before your partner does; as they keep trying all you can really do is offer your patience. Or perhaps you came into the relationship with a certain quality already developed that your partner is still working on.

Sara and I both love to grow, but we have come to learn that our journeys won't always match up. When we started going away to meditation courses, we quickly started seeing the value and impact of meditation. I was so impressed with the fact that my mind felt lighter and less cluttered that I wanted to take the experiment of meditation to another level and bring it into my daily life. The consistency of a daily meditation practice can help cement the positive changes in your life and take them even further. I started meditating two hours every day in March 2015. Sara was really intrigued and supportive, but she wasn't ready to incorporate it into her life yet as she felt with her full-time job and commute it would be too much. My schedule was much more flexible at the time.

The goal of meditating two hours a day came from my interest in doing a silent twenty-day meditation course; one of the requirements to be eligible was to do this consistently for two years. I had sat a few ten-day courses and really loved them, so I was curious as to what a twenty-day course would be like. I knew I had gained so much from meditating Vipassana, and I felt ready to dig deeper into my determination and bring this valuable technique into my daily life and prepare myself for a twenty-day course. I appreciated the systematic approach to gradual development and was glad that a path forward was laid out for me.

Sara and I had both expressed interest in meditating daily in the past, but our first attempts weren't successful. It's a really big commitment. This time, as the weeks went by she saw that I wasn't giving up and we had a deep conversation. She told me she wasn't yet ready to sit two hours a day and wanted to try one hour. She found her own goal and stuck to it.

At first there was a bit of tension between the two of us around us being in different spaces regarding meditation. We both loved it, but we needed to move at our own paces when it came to committing more time. It was challenging because we like moving at the same speed, but we had to learn to let it go and just accept that we were both doing what was right for our individual processes. After successfully incorporating an hour of meditation into every day for nine months, Sara saw for herself that it was possible to do with her schedule and that she still had time to relax and watch TV. Proving to herself a daily practice was feasible, in March 2016, Sara started meditating two hours a day. I could see that she felt great personal victory from figuring it out on her own and that wouldn't have happened if I had pressured her. I'm also really grateful Sara was so supportive and didn't ask me to wait for her to be ready.

This was an era of big changes for Sara and me. We had

a similar situation happen to us with marijuana. We both smoked during college. In our mid-twenties we started talking a lot about how we were tired of it and didn't really like it anymore. I had already stopped doing hard drugs by then, but I kept drinking and smoking and occasionally using psychedelics. Smoking weed was an integral part of our lives, something that we did daily, and it was a medium of communication for us and for how we relaxed and hung out. Smoking was there for us at the beginning of our relationship, so for a long time we didn't question it because it was so normal for us. I started noticing that weed was making my mind less sharp, and it was making me anxious. Sara noticed that it was making her exhausted, and it was giving her a feeling of being hungover.

After a few months of talking about it, we both decided together to stop smoking and see what life was like. To me the challenge felt pretty intense. I had not realized how much of my interactions with friends and life were mediated through smoking weed. It was a part of all situations that I considered fun at the time. During the break I noticed how much I relied on it for social situations. It felt like something was missing in most of my daily interactions. It was also a shock to friends who I would always smoke with. For them, and for me, smoking together felt like a quiet ritual among us, and not partaking in it felt like I was doing something wrong. I was afraid of not being part of the group because I was choosing something different. Not smoking was creating a lot of tension for me.

After a few months of no longer smoking, internally I felt pretty stressed out, but Sara was fine. In fact, she was loving it. She felt like her energy was better than ever and she was no longer weighed down by that feeling of being burned out. She was enjoying her mental clarity and her new sense of focus. Letting go of weed was not stressful for her. She was ready for this step in a way that I was not.

When we realized that we were in different places with this experiment it was tough. She liked developing a new way of being together without weed and I felt like I needed to go back to it. Honestly, I felt really uncertain. I liked the way smoking was part of my life, but I didn't like the way it made me feel. I liked the way it made social interactions easy, but I didn't like the way it would make me feel anxious when I smoked alone. After I weighed the way I liked it and didn't like it, I decided that I wanted to go back to smoking for a while to see what life was like with it once more. Sara wasn't happy with my decision, and in truth, I wasn't that happy with it either, but I was grateful that she gave me the space to go on my own journey.

I started smoking again and immediately I could feel that this was not for me; I really did not like the way it made me feel. I did it for a few months and I remember being quite grumpy through that experience. Why was I doing something that I didn't like? Was it just because the pattern was familiar? Yes. But I did learn a big lesson in those few months. The distaste I had for it was great enough that I knew it was worth taking on the challenge of finding new ways to connect with my friends, to not be afraid to do new things with them or to have deep conversations with them without having my mind in an altered state. I also learned that sometimes it takes falling back into a negative pattern to remember how over it we really are.

At that time I had already sat a few ten-day courses and I could see that meditation expanded my mind and enhanced my understanding of myself and the universe in a way that weed and psychedelics could not. Psychedelics felt like they would briefly expose me to some truths but when they wore off the truths seemed more like intellectual speculation than a genuine felt experience that was fully integrated in my being. Meditation left a much bigger, longer-lasting impact that was transforming my behaviors and clarifying my perception of the world. The universal truths I came across through meditation were life changing, and this vibrancy was maintained and enhanced as I started bringing meditation into my daily life.

Meditating felt like it was bringing me to incredible depths, and weed and psychedelics were keeping my mind at a certain density that I was ready to go beyond. Granted, this is my personal experience, but it feels right to write about them candidly. I tried smoking and various psychedelics before I tried meditation, and they were honestly mind expanding, but when I tried Vipassana meditation, it blew those experiences out of the water.

During the few months I went back to smoking, Sara was incredibly patient with me. It was a real challenge for both of us because we would spend time together, but our minds were going through different experiences. After some time, I knew that deep in my heart I was done with it and ready to build a new life without it. Sara quietly rejoiced when I told her and supported me as I navigated life without substances.

In both those experiences we were moving at different speeds and even though we both wanted to be in the same place it would have been dishonest and counterproductive to force ourselves to be in a place we were not ready for. I am grateful to our past selves for being open about how we really felt because it helped us build a culture between us that is ultimately more accepting and supportive of changes, even if they are not synchronous.

GROWING IN DIFFERENT WAYS

More often than not, one partner may be more interested in healing and self-development than the other. This is not a problem, but it is challenging to accept this reality. I have seen many partnerships over the years work beautifully, even when both people have really different hobbies and interests.

Even if your partner is not interested in meditation, therapy, or other forms of self-analysis, it does not mean they are doing life wrong. Everyone can benefit from cultivation, but that does not mean that we all need to cultivate ourselves through the same means. If your partner can do their part to create a nurturing and fulfilling environment, if you feel joy being in their presence and you trust them as your lover and best friend, then you don't need to be growing in the exact same ways.

The important thing is that if you feel like you can benefit from healing and developing yourself, then commit to it and walk the path even if no one is joining you for the ride. There is immense benefit in inner cultivation, and you will see the fruits of your labor in the way that it improves your mind, interactions with others, meaningful relationships, and life.

A loving partner will support you in what is good for you, even if they themselves are not partaking. You and your partner do not need to be twins to love each other well. You can support each other in your different endeavors and still have plenty of common ground in the loving home you have created together.

KNOWING YOUR PARTNER'S TRIGGERS

Understanding each other's triggers is necessary in a serious relationship. As you two get to know each other more and more, it will become clear that life has not been easy for either of you. No individual experiences life without having gone through some form of harm or developing some habits and patterns that are detrimental. Even at its most beautiful, life can be stressful. Trigger points are essentially moments or experiences of our past that heavily coat our present-day perception. When we encounter something like what we experienced in the past that reminds us of that dreadful moment, the same intense reaction surfaces as a coping mechanism or as a form of self-defense. Sometimes the defense is necessary and sometimes it is totally unwarranted because the mind perceives danger where there is none.

What is difficult is that we are not each other's therapists. We are not individuals trained to handle someone else's trauma. We are merely peers who love each other. All we can do is our best to understand the other's emotional terrain, to equip each other with as much information as possible about why we are the way we are. This is especially important for long-term relationships. Having the courage to walk each other through our emotional histories takes a lot of strength but it is necessary if we are to have a good chance at loving each other well.

Understanding someone's triggers does not mean tiptoeing around them or coddling them. It means being well-informed so that you can skillfully and gently hold each other's vulnerability when you are going through difficult moments or having deep conversations. When the heart is open during moments of vulnerability, it is valuable to remember your partner's trigger points so that you can treat each other compassionately.

When your partner decides to do healing work to overcome their triggers, make sure that you support them in moving at a pace that is good for them. This is not the time to "test" them in unnecessary ways. They should clearly outline what they are comfortable with and how they would like your help. You are not your partner's coach and, in fact, when trying to do deep healing work it is better to involve professionals so that you can successfully maneuver this sensitive process.

You can't force your partner to change or heal in the ways you want them to. Even though you may think you know what is best for them and you see a clear way for them to deal with their inner issues or old pain, it simply is not helpful to push someone to do work that only they themselves can decide they are ready for. Of course, you can give suggestions and share what has helped you, but every person needs to walk the path of healing themselves, from their own volition. Love is founded on freedom; this implies that you need to lean into your acceptance and patience if you are committed to growing together. No relationship is without conflict or difficult moments, especially because individuals grow and heal at different speeds. At the same time, nothing should be taken to an extreme. Realizing that you have waited long enough and that you would benefit from being alone or finding a new partner who has or is working toward the qualities you are looking for is something that needs to come from your own intuition and reasoning. The right action should emerge from within you and it should help bring balance to your life.

BUILDING, BREAKING, AND REGAINING TRUST

Trust is one of the main foundations of all relationships. A groundwork of trust permits us to open up and be vulnerable, allowing us to share our full, complex selves with another person. Trust means we won't feel judged or threatened when we admit a shortcoming or fear. Trust allows for humans to be imperfect beings and feel supported in the process of growing and making mistakes. Trust also means we can feel sure of our partner and their commitment to our relationship. It allows us to relax and feel at ease in our home and our lives. Trust creates space for more to be possible, more creativity, more growth, more joy, more contentedness.

But trust needs to be built and earned step by step in a gradual process shown by actions, rather than just words. As your relationship grows and builds, so should your trust in each other. There are so many ways to build trust, but the main one is to consistently show up for your partner in a caring and loving manner. To give them your attention, to listen to them, to accept them fully as they are, and to be there for them. Opening up to your partner with vulnerability is another way to build trust. When you can open yourself up to your partner despite the fear and tension it may bring up in you, you've created a huge opening for your relationship. Consistency is key to building trust.

Following through with what you have committed to do is essential. Being honest and not hiding things from your partner is paramount. This is important to establish early on in your relationship and applies even to small white lies. If you find yourself holding back or lying to your partner out of fear of hurting their feelings, you are actually hurting your bond more by not allowing full trust to develop.

When trust is absent or broken, it creates a dynamic of fear and insecurity that can cause tension and harm. This robs a relationship of its comfort and threatens the long-term viability of a partnership. If you cannot trust your partner, intimacy is lost and replaced by disappointment and fear. I have seen many great relationships end when trust is broken. It is good to have boundaries and not allow yourself to be mistreated, but at the same time, you shouldn't expect your partner to be perfect and never make mistakes.

I believe in many cases trust can be regained and rebuilt *if* both partners truly want this and work toward it patiently:

If responsibility is taken for the transgression, which often needs to happen a few times. If open and honest communication is reestablished. If you get to the root of why trust was broken, rather than just the surface level of what happened. If you can hold your partner with compassion and understanding, while not sanctioning their misdeeds. If you can see your partner as a beautifully complex and imperfect being who makes mistakes, but who owns up to them and learns from them. All of these conditions can lead to building an even deeper and stronger trust. But it will take time. *It is not a weakness to give your partner a second chance with accountability.* Though in some cases, especially when both partners do not want to put in the work, or the transgression is too deep, the relationship will not be salvageable.

If your trust has been broken in the past, this may cause you to have your guard up around others and expect them to hurt you in the same way. This pattern needs to be acknowledged and faced, communicated openly with your partner, and treated gently and patiently.

COMPARISON AND THE SOCIAL MEDIA EFFECT

The mind loves to compare and now that we live in the age of digital connection, the mind has more things to compare itself to than ever. This is not only dangerous for our mental health but can be detrimental to our relationships.

It is easy to forget that our friends, family, and the popular personalities we follow mainly share their highlight reels. The steady stream of information we get on our phones is often the best-of-the-best events and that can create deeply unrealistic expectations of what daily life should be like.

When you see videos of other people's relationships, all of the laughing and picture-perfect vacations, it can make you crave the same things in your life. Craving is not picky; it will grab any appealing idea, attach itself to it, and use it as a means to create tension in the mind.

The reality of relationships could not be more different from what you see online. Relationships have plenty of joyful moments, but they also have a lot of quiet, unexciting, and trying moments. Big promotions, beautiful trips, weddings, and major life updates get many more clicks and views than talking about the mundaneness of grocery shopping or the hardship of debt.

Constantly scrolling can make you underappreciate what you have and make you crave things that are totally unnecessary. And it can make you see gaps in your relationship that are just a figment of your imagination.

Additionally, when you are interested in personal growth and follow therapists and other self-help people, you have to be mindful not to try to put your relationship into a perfect process. Even with all that I am writing here, the purpose of it is not how to love perfectly; it is how to love better. And better will still contain messiness, down days, and a lack of clarity that someone outside of your relationship will not be able to resolve. It will be up to you and your partner to figure out solutions that will only work for the two of you. Don't try for perfection, try for improvement.

Be mindful of the terminology that becomes temporarily popular online. Therapeutic words can quickly become trendy and then the ego may try to weaponize them in conversation. Make sure that if you are using new terminology you both have a clear and shared understanding of it. Remember, if you don't understand each other, then it will be difficult to come to a new level of harmony.

There is a lot of beauty in relationship moments that will never go viral. Simple trips to the supermarket together, inside jokes that only the two of you can decipher, sitting silently on the couch, or just the small joy of discovering a new TV show are all more relationship-building than a staged sunset photo. Every moment does not need to be life-changing and blissful. If that is what you are expecting from a relationship, then you will miss many of the simple joys of being alive. The beauty of life happens in between the loud moments. If you can stop looking for highs and teach yourself to live and enjoy the present moment, you will find that your appreciation of your partner will reach a new level.

Don't try to copy another person's relationship. Even though social media makes it easy to crave what you are not currently experiencing, falling into the trap of craving what's not in front of you will consistently lead to dissatisfaction. Find a balance between appreciating your relationship for what it is and having conversations with your partner about things you can work on to keep evolving the love you have for each other.

Loving your partner well often looks
like moving at a slower speed
when they are feeling down.

You don't rush them to get over it.
You let them move through their emotions.
You ask them if they would like any help.
Meeting them where they are
supports their healing.

BEYOND THE ATTACHMENT TO PERFECTION

Striving to create a life of permanent external peace reveals a deep attachment to perfection and an aversion to unpleasant situations. It also reveals a lack of understanding of change, which is ever-present and all-pervasive. Since change is constantly happening, this opens the door to uncertainty, which will ultimately allow in some form of conflict, discomfort, or challenge.

When you deeply accept that change is always happening, it makes it easier to relinquish the fruitless pursuit of total control. This also points your attention inward and shows you that instead of spending your energy trying to control the outer world, there is the need to build the habit of managing your reactions within. So that when things do become chaotic, you can feel the truth of your temporary emotions while simultaneously choosing to remain in your peace.

Two things can help your
nervous system:

Being around kindhearted
and self-aware people

Developing the inner
balance to not react to
everything around you

There are too many unknowns and uncontrollable factors in the outside world, which means it is not a canvas that is solely yours to paint. But you can know yourself well enough to make your mind a home that is intentionally designed to have a foundation of gentleness and compassion.

Tough emotions will come and go freely, but knowing the truth about change should help to manage your reactions in a way that enables you to slow down, not jump to conclusions or spiral out of control. This allows you to figure out what is the most skillful way to deal with the challenges that arise instead of just repeating past defensive behaviors that usually bring you more difficulty.

The wise do not hurry, nor do they try to control everything; instead they move intentionally and understand that impulsive reactions function as a barrier to their peace.

Reflection Questions

- What are the main challenges your relationships have faced? The next time these challenges arise, how can you address them more productively?
- Are you pulling your weight when facing relationship challenges?
- Are you and your partner communicating calmly and well when in the midst of a challenge?
- Does this partnership have enough trust that you can be vulnerable and let down your guard? If not, are there steps you can take to build up that trust?
- Do you fall into the trap of comparing your relationship to picture-perfect ones online? How can you break out of this habit?

chapter 9

When to Break Up

Some of the hardest moments in life are when you have to decide whether the relationship you are in is right for you. Knowing if or when to break up can be challenging because the advice you get from the trusted people in your life is simply a perspective you take into consideration. The ultimate decision is one you need to make for yourself because only you know the intricate aspects of the relationship and you are the one who can feel the truth of your heart. Those outside the relationship can only get a glimpse, they will never have the direct experience of the issues and challenges that you and your partner are facing.

Breaking up is a life-changing moment. It is a time when you decide to overhaul a big portion of your life and start fresh. It is not a decision that is made lightly. Every relationship is so unique, they are each their own world and one is never exactly the same as another. This uniqueness means that each breakup has its own set of causes. To make such a big decision requires moments of serious introspection so you can be sure your decision is aligned with what is best for you.

Here are six things to consider as you think through your decision:

1. **When the discord is relentless and unending.** If it always feels like there is no harmony or joy in your relationship, then something is really off. Relationships are never going to be perfect; they always have their ups and downs. The difference here is if it consistently feels like you are moving from one down moment to another. When joy and happiness feel scarce and hard to come by, it will be difficult to genuinely feel safe or at home in a relationship. Love comes with its challenges, but it should also come with a feeling of uplift, deep connection, and empowerment.

2. **When your intuition is persistently telling you that this is not the right match for you.** Intuition usually arrives as a feeling, and it will continue arising until you follow its guidance or until you fully suppress it. Intuition is our inner compass; it helps us live a life of learning and fulfillment. If it repeatedly feels like this relationship is not for you, then this is something worth considering. This may even happen when someone is a good person and partner, but they may not be the right one for you.

3. **When they no longer feel right in your arms.** The body sometimes knows before the mind does. When your body no longer wants to be close to theirs, this is a signal that needs to be considered. Even for two people who love each other but are not very affectionate, there will still be a sense of comfort and correctness while they are in each other's presence.

4. **When growth and evolution are not a priority.** A lot of relationships go through tough moments when one or both partners realize they need to change their actions to help support the harmony of the relationship. Relationships shine a mirror on each individual and show the ways they need to grow. The struggle comes when one partner, or both, makes little or no effort to evolve. If the relationship feels like a constant storm and no one is trying to make things better, or you are the only one consistently putting in effort, then you might have gone as far as you can with this partnership.

5. **When you can't be vulnerable with them.** Someone who loves you should be very interested in your emotions and should be excited to get to know more about you, even if you are unveiling the hard parts of your story. Vulnerability creates closeness and without it you two will remain far away from each other. If your partner is not open to your vulnerability, if you feel like you can't

share your truth with them, then it will not be possible to feel at home with them. It can feel quite lonely when your partner does not want to hear about your emotions and inner self.

6. **When it feels like life is moving you in different directions.** There are some relationships that are meant to last for a chapter of your life, but not for your entire story. This happens often when people have to move for work or school. There are also big life changes that can arise that make us dramatically switch our priorities. Sometimes it feels like someone fits well in one phase of your life, but not when a new one opens. There are even times when individuals continue growing, but their inner changes no longer click as well as when they initially met. It is okay to accept that you have grown apart or are now in different and incompatible phases of your lives.

The energy is:

Love me well or leave me alone.

Before you can make a full decision about whether to break up or not you first need to make sure that you are not throwing away a good relationship because you are craving a perfect one. Craving has an insidious and potent effect on the mind; it will cause you to look at the life you have and make it seem insufficient.

Craving is a hunger that can never be fully quenched. When you fall under the influence of craving, it can make you think your partner is not enough when in reality they are a fantastic person. Craving loves to combine itself with the attachment to perfection. It will make you chase a picture-perfect life, but the danger here is that you may end up throwing away a life that others dream of just so you can seek perfection.

Craving will make you look for something better and easier. It will tempt you to look at challenges in a relationship as roadblocks. It will even make you forget that much of the beauty you enjoy from a relationship comes after the two of you overcome a storm together. In the midst of a moment of struggle, the two of you will actually get an opportunity to get to know each other better and a chance to understand that your love for each other is more important than an argument.

Craving is a naturally selfish emotion that needs to be treated thoughtfully and maturely. Even seemingly positive aspirations, such as leaving a relationship to pursue growth and development, can be overly selfish and rooted in craving. You don't have to be alone or with a person walking a very similar path to be able to make progress within yourself. Make sure you are not using this as an excuse to get out of responsibility or a situation you no longer want to be in. It is so important to be honest with ourselves and our partners about the root reasons we want to leave a relationship and not cover them up with outwardly noble causes.

Love is not:

Feeling nervous often,
chaos, insecurity, and the
excitement of the chase

Love is:

Clarity, feeling seen, calm
attention, and knowing
that you are committed
to each other

Before you decide to break up, make sure your mind is arriving at this conclusion from a balanced place. Trying to find a new partner that is just a little bit better is often a big mistake. Continuously pursuing the thrill of the honeymoon phase of a new relationship will not lead to lasting contentment. This can become an endless chase where you end up seeking the feeling of newness as opposed to the feeling of genuine depth. Newness comes with the feelings of elation, a strong high, and excitement, but that initial phase does not reveal the true value of a relationship. Ultimately, only you know whether your decision is born from craving or from a genuine need to start a new life that is undoubtedly better for you.

There are different ranges of discord that can arise in a relationship; it can go from normal and natural discord to incompatibility and all the way to abuse. Incompatibility may not be clear until you actually act on what feels like a genuine connection. Once you start spending intentional time with each other, there may be big differences in your personal and cultural upbringings that make it feel like you are never quite understanding each other, or you may just not be right for each other. Your personalities and perspectives never quite align and what one of you perceives as normal may be totally new and unwanted for the other. This clash of differences creates an unsustainable and sometimes uncomfortable environment until one of you decides it's time to walk away. Incompatibility does not come from a place of malice because no one is intending to do harm, but more so from both individuals living in mindsets and worlds that do not overlap well. Intention is the key here.

The other matter that needs to be mentioned is feeling unsafe in a relationship. When you feel emotionally or physically unsafe, this is a clear sign that it is time to move on, even if there are deep feelings involved. There is no good reason to tolerate abuse, even if you are hoping or waiting for your partner to change. Waiting for your abuser to change is an exceedingly dangerous mindset. In these cases, it is best to remove yourself from the situation or call for support from people you love and trust to help you step away from a relationship that is harmful. Preserving your mental health and personal safety are foundational elements of self-love and self-care.

It is hard to stay in a relationship
with someone who does not see
the way they project the tension in their mind
into their daily interactions.

It is common to consult those closest to you before a breakup. Family and close friends are certainly some of the people who know us best, but it is important to remember that no one knows your situation as well as you do. It can be helpful to say out loud what has been in your mind. But whether to break up or not is sometimes a matter of closing your eyes and deeply listening to your intuition. It will let you know which direction to move in. Having confidence in yourself and trusting yourself to be your own leader is a valuable quality to develop.

TEMPORARY AND MEANINGFUL

Some of the most meaningful relationships do not last a lifetime. They are moments when we become so deeply entwined with another individual that it sparks profound growth and gives us vital direction as we move forward in life. Sometimes you share a chapter of your life with an individual so you can both get through a serious hurdle. You were not meant to be together for a lifetime, but you were meant to help each other reach a new level. Our society tends to give bigger meaning to relationships that last for longer lengths of time, and without taking away from the beauty of these partnerships, this is not always the truth. Even relationships that last for weeks or months can leave an undeniable impact on the mind and the heart. No love or care that you received is lost. Just as past difficulties continue to impact you, so does past love. What matters is not time, but the depth of the connection and how the connection affected that specific chapter of your life.

Even when you go your separate ways, there is an unforgettable kinship that was forged. It happens often that someone feels genuinely right for a moment in time, but then a shift happens as your life goes from one chapter to another.

Real love contains a timeless quality. You can feel this in the moments when you and another person are so deeply enjoying each other's company that time seems to slow down though it is actually moving quickly without you even noticing it. It is as if you two enter your own realm and what feels like minutes for the both of you is hours in the outside world. This is a profound act of presence that becomes more doable when you love someone deeply. You give them so much of your attention that it feels like time stops as you listen and engage in conversation with them. These are special moments when your connection unfolds and becomes truly alive, when you can feel the magnetic pull of the spark that brings the two of you together. When you see the power of love in a single moment, it makes it easier to understand that a temporary relationship can have a powerful impact on your mind and heart. Even when the two of you reach a fork in the road and go your separate ways, you can look back on the story of your life and honestly admit to yourself that this union was formative and supportive in your development as a human being.

Whether you consider a short relationship you were in as negative or positive, there is still so much value you can gain from what you went through. Many of us have relationships or parts of relationships we regret, but even though we can't turn back time or erase that relationship from our mind, there is still value to gain. Undesirable relationships can show you what you don't want to repeat in the future and help you clarify what type of qualities you are looking for in a partner. Understanding what you should not tolerate is essential. The hurt you felt in the past can be transmuted into healing and growth, but it can also clarify your inner compass so you know what is good for you and what isn't. Looking back on a relationship you regret and realizing how things went wrong can help you build a much more generative relationship culture with a future partner. In a very direct way, what we don't like will help us welcome what we do like.

DRAGGING ON

It often takes time to figure out if someone you are with is no longer right for you. Sometimes you may even need the information of having more experiences with them before you can really see if moving forward together in life is the right thing for you.

A common occurrence is that even once the answer is clear in our hearts, we still don't make a move to end the relationship and we let it drag on. Living in this state of being in a relationship that you know is not meant to last is painful. In these moments, life feels like a contradiction, the mind feels heavy with tension, and your interactions with your partner start to feel halfhearted.

It takes a lot of courage to intentionally close a chapter of your life so you can open another. When two people are together they deeply intertwine their lives, especially if the relationship has lasted for years and maybe children are involved. Experiencing life together can feel like the safe thing to keep doing simply because that is what you know. Some people stay in a relationship they don't like just because it feels comfortable to do so. You accept the comfort over choosing the challenge of rebuilding a more aligned life. Even when you know intuitively that there is a better life waiting for you, it takes a lot of determination to intentionally step into the unknown.

There are also relationships where there is nothing immensely wrong about how your partner treats you, but you can just feel it in your being that they are not the one for you. In these moments it requires compassion to fully end the relationship so you can both move forward. Things need to break so they can be replaced by something better.

Letting an incompatible relationship drag on is an injustice to yourself and your partner. Even if you live for a hundred years, a human life is very short when compared to cosmological time scales. Burning up your time with someone you don't feel is right for you is unfair to you and to them. Because you care for them, you should end the relationship in a clear and kind manner where no one is left confused. Letting things drag on for months or years simply stops the both of you from moving on.

Someone can love you deeply,
but if they don't have the emotional skills
to care for the relationship
it will be a rough road.

THE SPLIT

Once you have carefully and thoughtfully decided it is the right decision to end a relationship, going about it in the best way possible is paramount. Trying to be as compassionate as possible as you break up is a really challenging but worthwhile goal. The truth of the breakup is difficult enough, and when skillfully handled can facilitate a faster and easier healing process for both of you. Trying not to attack your partner's character or make this entirely their fault can be really helpful. Strive to speak the truth about your decision honestly but calmly, knowing there are two sides to every story. Even trying to validate that you admire and have love for them, but that they are just not the right person for you, or it's not the right time, can be a great path forward. It's not easy to let someone else down, someone who we cared for, but that shouldn't keep us from moving forward with the path we think is best. Gather your courage and be bold in following your intuition.

Reflection Questions

- Do you put your partner's needs above your own in your relationship?
- What is your strategy for removing yourself from a situation that is no longer conducive to your happiness and well-being?
- Is there room for you to love yourself more within your relationship? How?
- How can you go about a breakup without causing more harm, how can you approach this situation sensitively and compassionately?
- Are you scared to move on even though you know it is the right move?

chapter 10

Recovering from Heartbreak

Living with an open heart, one that is emotionally ready for connection, is bound to come with risks. When you fall in love and start the process of building a deep bond with another human being, love becomes more than a feeling, it becomes an energy that shapes and molds your life. When a partnership ends, especially when the ending is unwanted, the sting of having to create a new way of existing is significant and sometimes overwhelming.

Not only do you have to deal with the material changes like altering your daily routine that used to be deeply entangled with your former partner, but you also have to deal with the heavy emotions that come with a breakup.

When two lives that have intentionally moved alongside each other for a long period of time decide to go their separate ways, hurt is bound to come up because you are forced to let go of the parts of your identity that were connected to your relationship. Loving and being loved by a specific person can become an identity you attach yourself to. Facing loneliness and missing someone, who may or may not have been good for you, is natural because they were a big part of your life. Removing a loved one from our hearts often wounds our egos, which react defensively to protect us. Together no longer, you are forced to reassess and rebuild what home means within yourself. Together no longer, you have no other choice but to go beyond your comfort zone and enter into the unknown.

Even though the pain is substantial there are four key realizations that will help you feel renewed:

1. **Your time was not wasted**. The energy you used building patience, speaking up for yourself, setting boundaries, having difficult conversations, improving your ability to communicate your emotions—all of these are valuable qualities that will support every part of your life. Having a partner often creates the conditions for you to get to know yourself more deeply, to see the behavior patterns you were once unaware of, and to better understand your triggers. A partnership, whether harmonious or not, will function like a mirror. The combination of seeing yourself clearly and accepting the challenge of growth will help you become a more socially skillful individual in the long run. If you look at your former relationship through the right lens, there will be plenty there for you to study and learn. Realizing the value you

gained out of something that ended can be deeply healing.

2. **Let yourself grieve the loss of the relationship but remind yourself that this is not the end of the world.** The pain is real but just like everything else in this universe, it is impermanent. Heartache can simply not last forever, it will have its highs and lows, moments when you feel it more strongly than others, but if you use this as an opportunity for rebirth, your grief will become fuel for your evolution. Allow your sorrow to point you in the direction of the home that you need to strengthen within yourself. Don't suppress your emotions, give them space to breathe, observe them, feel them, let them move through you, but don't attach yourself to them.

3. **What are you looking for that you can give yourself?** Heartache should initiate a period of self-love. This is a time when you can become a better friend to yourself. Ask yourself: "How can I treat myself better?" and follow through on activating the love you are missing from within. Building a home within yourself is not just about self-acceptance; it is also about reinforcing habits and understandings that help you feel at peace in your solitude. Feeling full while alone means there is no longer distance between you and yourself. Use the heavy emotions you feel as a medium to connect more deeply with

yourself. Remember, the relationship you have with yourself is the longest and most impactful relationship you will ever have in your life.

4. **The value of friendship.** When a relationship gets serious, a lot of your energy is placed into it and unconsciously that energy is taken from other connections with friends and family. This is not done out of malice or carelessness, and most often it is simply because it takes a lot of time to build a partnership, and time is not limitless. The lesson many people learn during periods of heartbreak is that it is healthier to consistently feed your friendships, whether you are in a relationship or not, because great fulfillment comes from community. Every individual in your life will help bring out a unique side of you, and this gets stunted when you center your life around just one individual. Let your friends know you appreciate them, let them support you and find ways to help them when they need it. Friendships are some of the most nourishing connections you will experience in your life.

Reframe heartbreak into a moment of rebirth,
an opening to a new and better you.

Feel the sadness, but don't let it stop you
from learning and evolving.

Stand in your power,
gather your self-worth,
and walk forward into a better life.

Since a breakup is literally a break, the end of a chapter in your life, the only real option is to let this become a moment of rebirth for you. This is clearly a time of sorrow, but it can also be one where you unflinchingly stand in your power. The hurt is real but so is the potential for you to emerge as a restored and revitalized version of yourself.

The first major step is acceptance; even though this may not be what you want, this is the reality, and it has to be accepted that this breakup is happening. It takes two willing people to be in a relationship and if one no longer wants it to continue for whatever reason, you can't force it to happen. Fighting this reality will prolong your pain and not allow you to move forward. The sooner you can accept this truth into your heart and being, the sooner you can start healing and moving on. Though our mind may cling to this strong attachment of the relationship, we have to be honest with ourselves and accept that what we used to be attached to is no longer there for us in the same way and we need to let go. Accepting this truth is the first vital step in moving forward and healing.

After the breakup, it's important to soothe yourself back into calmness so you can realign and reconnect with your inner stability. This may take days, weeks, or even months, it all depends on how long you were together and the amount of hurt you feel. Remember, even if you were the one who initiated the breakup, you can still feel plenty of grief and a sense of loss. If you were on the receiving end of the breakup, this can shake you even more deeply. Either way, the need for healing and moving forward is clear in both situations.

Remind yourself that you are not permanently broken and that your value as a human being is not in question. Feelings of unworthiness are common in this state, but you should not believe them. Your value is not determined by what other people think of you; your value is a wellspring that emerges from within. The emotional heaviness, the tears, the loneliness, the feeling of regret, all this turbulence will not last forever.

As you regain your footing and get a little more comfortable with this new chapter, it is worth asking yourself some serious questions. Use self-reflection as a way to learn more about yourself: What went wrong? How can you do things better in the future? This is the time for you to redirect your story. Use this as a period of self-reflection so you can walk forward with new wisdom that helps you to be more intentional in life.

Six Questions for Self-Reflection After a Breakup

1. **What narratives have you been holding on to that are not serving you well?** The stories in your mind that used to bind together your old relationship should be intentionally released. You can certainly live a great life

without your former partner. You are strong enough to redesign your life into something beautiful. Any narrative where you see yourself needing them to thrive is untrue.

2. **Were you looking for the wrong qualities in a partner?** Sometimes there are characteristics we find attractive, ones we gravitate toward, but once we are close with the person, we find that these traits do not help in building a fulfilling home together. What qualities are needed in a relationship that you should be looking for instead?

3. **What behaviors did you have in your former relationship that you will not bring into a future relationship?** No one is perfect and relationships make this blaringly clear. Whether we initiated the breakup or not, we certainly have qualities that can create friction. This is not meant for you to be overly critical of yourself, it is simply a practice in honesty so that you can move forward with greater self-awareness. Being able to see your rough points is the first step in overcoming them.

4. **Are you giving yourself enough time to heal?** There is a lot of power and growth in letting yourself spend some time with just yourself. Jumping from one relationship to another, without any substantial space in between, makes it hard to see that you alone are the creator

of your inner happiness. Spending time tending to your inner garden can set you up for a new era of flourishing.

5. **Did you feel empowered in your last relationship?** It can feel wondrous to build a life with another human being, but in that process, it is important to not lose yourself as an individual. It is good for you to have your own preferences, interests, likes, and dislikes. Two people who love each other are not obligated to constantly move together as one or to always have the same opinions. The differences actually make the relationship sweeter and deeper if you both embrace them. Now that the relationship has ended, can you refocus on your individual interests and passions?

6. **Can you find joy as an individual?** This one is especially important, because if we cannot see the beauty in life as we walk the earth alone, that means there is some internal disconnection. Using self-awareness and self-love to close the gap between you and yourself will make every part of life more vibrant. Befriend yourself, be your own student and teacher, practice being in the moment, don't run from your emotions, let yourself enjoy nature and silence.

In a time when people devalue kindness,
let your heart remain wide open.
Keep giving your gentleness to the world.
Act with kindness without worrying
about what you will get in return.

Even if people forget what you did for them,
the universe won't.

I've both gone through breakups and witnessed many friends and family members go through breakups. These can be challenging times, especially when we are expected to carry on with work and life like everything is fine. Living together, sharing finances and children all make breakups more difficult, and I've seen these sensitive times handled with both grace and bitterness. Losing the love and support from the person closest to us causes enough pain, so we should do all we can to not make it a more painful process. Though our egos may be hurt, we should do our best to not act out of resentment or animosity. Being petty often comes from a place of being hurt and sad and will not ultimately make us feel better; rather it just attempts to bring down another person and keeps us down in turn. And if we do take it too far in the heat of the moment, we should apologize. We once loved this person; perhaps we still do. To be able to continue to treat them with love and respect is an incredible sign of maturity. It is possible to grieve and protect your heart in these moments and still treat others with kindness.

Healing from Heartbreak

Here are six considerations that can help the healing process:

1. **Simple steps forward are a victory.** Sorrow makes time slow down. Sometimes this feels painful because the

common inclination is to want to rush into a new and better life, but slowing down can become a productive tool. You don't want to run from the pain, because that will just make it multiply in your subconscious and it will impact your behavior patterns in a negative way. Instead, you want to walk mindfully through each day, without avoiding what arises within you but simultaneously not allowing sorrow to govern your actions. Simply being with your emotions without becoming them is a victory that should not be overlooked. These slow and intentional steps with your emotions can also be transferred to other aspects of your life. Each positive action that uplifts your heart, each conversation with a friend that reminds you that there is still plenty of beauty to enjoy in life, each time you remember that every moment of life is a new beginning—these are all simple steps forward that will reinvigorate you.

2. **Let your healing take the time it needs.** There is no perfect formula for healing and no precise amount of time that it takes to mend the heart and mind. With healing, time is not even the major factor. What matters most is that you are putting energy into unpacking, understanding, and unbinding the heavy conditioning and hurt you carry. Through meditation, journaling, therapy, or intentional living, you will find a process that helps you feel renewed and lighter. Make sure that rushing or forcing is

not part of your plan; quickness is not a sign of healing or strength. Let the ups and downs be a natural part of your journey; don't fight the fact that not every day will be a great day. Be patient with yourself. Let yourself breathe into each moment. Keep directing your life with the magic of your intention; this will help you find your way forward.

3. **Apply what you have learned.** If you look closely, heartbreak and endings always come with lessons. Whether it is the ending of a good chapter or one you regret, there should still be ample knowledge for you to integrate. Seeing a harmful pattern of yours and doing nothing to transmute it into more skillful behavior that supports your happiness and power is where many get stuck. Be honest with yourself, learn how your past impacts your present, but then use this information to enact targeted changes that make your life brighter. Relationships will often expand your understanding of love, but understanding is not enough; what you learn should refine the way you practice love.

4. **Reconnect with gratitude.** It is easy to get lost in sorrow, to only repeat in your mind what has gone wrong and to lose sight of all the good in your life. Even though the hurt is real and deep, and creating a new life for yourself is a hard task, taking moments to genuinely re-

member there are things to be grateful for can help balance your mind. Think of the way you can nourish your body with food and water, the sunlight that brightens your day, how far you have come in your growth and resiliency, and the friendships that lift you up—there are plenty of things to remind you that there is beauty and magic in your life.

5. **Put down your defenses.** Coming back from heartbreak can feel like an uphill battle. Not only do you have to find ways to nurture your heart back into a sense of balance, but you also have to mindfully bring your defenses down so new connections have the opportunity to flourish. *The behaviors that once protected you while you were with someone who did not know how to properly care for your heart can end up becoming walls that stop you from letting a new partner love you well.* The hurt of heartbreak can make us hesitant to try again and risk this same pain. It is a struggle to not revert to survival mode. The difficulty of life makes it easy to lean on defensive-behavior patterns but living like this can make life lose its vibrancy.

6. **Understand that change is not your enemy; it is an opportunity.** Embracing change is one of the biggest lessons that all human beings are learning. Normally, our relationship with change is a combative one, where we simply want to keep everything we like the same. Even

when life repeatedly shows us that it is impossible to keep everything tranquil and perfect, we will still strive to control as much as we can in the hopes that life may remain pleasurable. Breakups are one of the major ruptures that the heart can experience, but this is not always a loss. If anything, it is a clear sign that something was wrong and that this is an opening that you must use to create a better life. You must remind yourself that your true power is expressed by the decisions you make. You can't control the world, but you can design your life through your deliberate choices.

Reflection Questions

- Are you letting yourself feel the grief and sadness without getting swept away by them?
- Are you being patient with your healing process and leaning on practices that support this transition in your life? What practices could you lean into more?
- Now is a great time to focus on self-love. What are some ways you can show yourself some love, care, and attention?
- An ended relationship does not always mean a failure—are you able to not take it too personally?
- What lessons have you learned from the ended relationship?

chapter 11

Finding the Right Partner

Relationships built on beauty and lust alone do not have the foundation for a long-lasting union. Much more is needed to build a home. Falling in love with a person means being attracted to their mannerisms, their resilience, their brilliance and humor, the way they move about in the world, the decisions they make, their aspirations and values, and, most important, the way their being feels naturally right sitting next to yours—these are qualities that are not normally visible on the surface. It takes wanting to know someone at a deeper level to fully see how special they are.

You may fall in love with someone for who they are in that moment, but mature relationships have space for each person to grow and evolve. The person you fall in love with initially will not remain the same throughout the entirety of your relationship. If the connection is strong and your commitments have created a safe and rejuvenating relationship, then it won't be hard to fall in love with each other again and again. Part of loving each other well means getting to know the new aspects of your partner as they emerge. Loving your partner for who they are now, instead of the person you initially met, keeps the relationship fresh and focused on the present.

Your nervous system relaxes
around people who have:

Peace in their eyes
Growth in their plans
Kindness in their speech
Compassion in their perception
Emotional maturity in their decisions

It is important to be flexible when starting a relationship because only seeking perfection or checking off a list won't allow you to appreciate each individual. At the same time, it is essential to balance this truth with making sure to not lower your basic standards when it comes to new connections. Emotional availability, good communication, and clear effort are vital elements when seeing if someone is right for you. Even the beginnings of these qualities can be something you can work with if the person is showing a clear commitment to growth. Developing emotional maturity is truly a lifelong project. Especially when you understand that "doing the work" is both for the partnership and for inner development. No one has it all figured out and those of us who care about growth are in the midst of developing the habits we need to show up as the best versions of ourselves.

Many relationships don't begin with both people having a strong base of emotional maturity, especially those that start from a young age. It will become more common in the future as healing becomes an integral part of our global culture, but right now it is more about being open to growing together in a nourishing and sustainable manner. It is unreasonable to expect perfection from yourself or another person, but you can look for qualities that a healthy relationship can be built on, like humility, openness to feedback, and being in touch with one's emotions. Humility is necessary because without it, growth is not possible. Being open to feedback is valuable because through mutual honesty you create a safe and vibrant home together. Being in touch with your emotions is necessary because you need to know and accept yourself deeply to be able to love your partner well.

Another great quality to look for is the ability and genuine desire to commit. With so much at our fingertips and the chance for endless connections, some people have a hard time settling down because they are spoiled for choice. Not wanting to commit to any one person shows that they are stuck in a loop of continuously craving something new and exciting, like the honeymoon phase, and resisting the more serious and challenging parts of a relationship that lead to deeper intimacy. This is not someone you can fix or build a strong foundation with. This is something they need to figure out for themselves, and you should not take it personally or get involved. It's true that the honeymoon phase does not last forever and relationships are full of different eras and down times, but the consistent, reliable love and deep sense of security you get from commitment far outweighs this temporary high.

Goal:

No more forcing.
Let your energy speak for itself;
it will attract the right people
and good situations.

Focus on showing up as
the realest version of yourself
and things will align.

INTUITION HELPED ME FIND MY WIFE

The summer after my sophomore year in high school was a pensive one. I started reflecting on my life and realized how poverty was the source of my struggle and my family's. It hit me then that I needed to find a way to pull myself and my family out of what felt like the endless hamster wheel of poverty. In my young mind there were only two options to make money. I could do what some people around me were doing and join a gang to make money illicitly, but I knew that this came with serious drawbacks. I already knew this was a dangerous life, and I could see the way it ruined the lives of other young people in my community—this was a life that could easily lead to an early death or jail. The other option was to go to college and get a degree and find a way to make money afterward. Fortunately, I resolved on the second option mainly because life was already hard enough.

In my junior year, a friend of mine was the first person to tell me about Wesleyan University in Connecticut. I didn't really look into it much, but I did remember the name. When I started applying for schools in senior year the name really stuck with me, and it had its own advantages. It seemed like the best school that I could possibly get into. It was also close enough to Boston that I could come back home and visit my family, but far away enough where I could really get a new experience.

I ended up getting into many of the schools I applied to,

but my choice came down to two places, Wesleyan or Tufts. College was new to my family: the way the system worked in regard to studying for the SATs, visiting schools, applying for financial aid. And not only did it feel new to me; I also had to navigate it all on my own. I genuinely did not know you were supposed to visit universities before you picked one. Even though I had never been to the Wesleyan or Tufts campuses, I felt I had to pick between these two because they were the best schools I had gotten into. The offer from Tufts said I could attend for two hundred dollars a year without any loans. For Wesleyan I had to pay two thousand dollars a year and take out a few thousand dollars more in loans after financial aid. I knew Tufts was clearly the better financial offer, but my intuition was just not accepting it. My mind kept thinking about Wesleyan, and my whole being felt a magnetic pull to that school, even though I had never visited! Even though I was daunted by the cost, I picked Wesleyan. A few months later, after my decision was made, I finally visited the school. Everything I saw was so new and honestly a bit bewildering because campus life seemed starkly different from inner-city Boston where I grew up. While visiting the school I felt so much fear, and I kept thinking, "What the heck have I gotten myself into?" but even so I stuck with my intuition. It was clear that this experience was going to be hard but if I followed through, it would help me create the best life possible for myself and my family.

The way my intuition pulled me to Wesleyan felt otherworldly, and I am so deeply grateful that I listened, accepted the challenge, faced my fears, and walked into the unknown. Not only did I meet a lot of my closest friends there, learn a ton, and have some excellent teachers, but most important, I met Sara there.

To this day I feel like that pull to go to Wesleyan was by far the most critical move that my intuition has ever made. Like a compass, my intuition helped me find my wife. If I had not listened and instead moved with my fears and chosen an easier path, I might not have encountered Sara in this lifetime. If I had never met her, this book and my writing would not exist because she has been instrumental in everything I have created, both as a source of inspiration and for giving me her support to develop my craft as a writer. Without her, my life would be exceedingly different, and I am sure it would not be as fulfilling.

It took many different moments over years of me listening to my intuition before I was standing right in front of my wife. When I was finally there, my intuition became even more of a magnet, pulling us closer together and giving us many opportunities through our initial friendship to realize that we wanted to be together. Being drawn to her felt magical and necessary. Even though I would sometimes fight the pull that we had, I eventually let myself flow with it, and I could not be more grateful to my past self for listening and facing fear and uncertainty head-on.

What was especially interesting was that many of the internal issues that I needed to work on and the love of my life all appeared while I was in the same location. The same way that I would try to run away from my heavy emotions, I tried at times to run away from our relationship because I knew that if I was to be with her the only choice I really had was to heal myself, grow into a better version of myself, and do my best to be a better partner.

Partnership is one of the biggest gateways to growth; looking into her eyes and seeing that I had to face myself so we could have a better relationship was incredibly hard. It took me a few tries to fully settle into our relationship and a lot of that was because I was hovering around accepting that I had to do a lot of work within myself. I am grateful my intuition led me straight to my greatest challenge and to the best partner I could imagine.

As you look for your own partner, here are a few qualities that can help you decipher who is the right person for you to build a home with.

INTUITION

When looking for your person you should never undervalue the signs coming from your intuition. Do you feel the click? Does this person in front of you feel correct? Does your body feel a resounding *yes* when you are next to them?

Your intuition will bring you the unquantifiable information you need to prosper, and it will help you parse through all the people you encounter in your life so that you can give your time to the right ones. This is evermore true with social media connecting us with more people than in the past.

It is sometimes hard to trust your intuition because its workings are mysterious, personal, and occasionally the accuracy of the direction feels rooted in trusting yourself. When thinking about how much I had to go through and how many decisions I had to make to get the opportunity to meet my wife, it feels absolutely baffling, like there was an unseen line of causes and effects that was in play to help the situation for our meeting come into existence.

Goal:

No more lowering basic standards
and no more tolerating mistreatment.

Give your time to people who are
revitalizing and emotionally prepared
for deep connection.

Even though the origins of intuition may seem unclear, the effect it has on our lives is quite powerful if we listen to it. Intuition is literally your inner compass; it is a tool that will help you move in the direction of your well-being, and it will help you meet your goals. The purpose of intuition is not to make your life easy; rather it is meant to help give you direction, to help you grow, to help with the unraveling of what makes you feel heavy and the development of the inner qualities that will help your life shine more brightly. Intuition will ask you to face situations that may be quite far from your comfort zone. It will ask you to step into spaces you fear so you may conquer that fear and continue evolving. You can't overcome something without facing it head-on.

Intuition is not a voice or a being, it is the tool that helps your good karma come to fruition, it is the sharpened understanding of what is good for you and what is not. All the data you have gathered and the deep goals you have made form into a compass of clarity that will keep pushing you in a positive direction.

Intuition will never put you in danger and it will not ask you to harm yourself or others, but it will ask you to relinquish the way you cling to comfort, and it will challenge you to take new paths so your life can see different results. Intuition is the ultimate congregation of information that is not intellectualized but arrives as a calming and felt experience. It brings in the sharpness of what is right and not right.

Finally entered the phase where I just
want to be around kind people who
keep it real and love to grow.

The only people I think are cool now are those
who focus on building emotional intelligence,
unbinding past trauma, and gaining insight
through self-awareness.

When it comes to people, intuition is exceedingly useful because it helps connect you with some main characters in the great story of your life. As each chapter unfolds, as you strike upon each new adventure, you can always close your eyes and feel if you are going in the right direction and speaking with the right people.

There are countless numbers of people who you will find physically attractive, but coming upon a person who has something more, someone who your intuition says to stop and speak with, take a deeper look, see what you feel when you are standing next to them—this is the type of guidance that can make a huge difference in your life, but it will only have a positive effect if you are bold enough to act on the calming clarity of its message. Intuition will let you know who you should give your time to, and it will make it hard to run away from someone who is right for you.

A simple and consistent rule is if it does not click with your intuition, it is a no, thank you. Even if you live a very long life, time is limited; this creates a situation where you need to be intentional with your energy. Saying yes to projects and people who you feel halfhearted about will cause you an unnecessary amount of exhaustion and frustration. Make sure that when you say yes, you are saying yes with your whole heart.

Find a partner who is open to healing their emotional history because over time they will love you better and better.

Past pain can block love; fortunately your mutual commitment to your relationship energizes you both to address the burdens you have been carrying.

Letting go is hard, healing takes time, living in a new way requires courage.

You both offer your patience and support to each other because you know this emotional investment will yield incredible results.

As peace expands within your individual hearts, your relationship starts glowing with a fresh vibrancy.

You never strive for perfection; instead you embrace realness.

You communicate your ups and downs instead of projecting, you do your best to handle conflict calmly, you apologize when you make mistakes.

You both accept the challenge of this new adventure because the love you share is worth it.

PROXIMITY AND EMBODIMENT

People have different strategies when it comes to finding a partner. Some feel inclined to actively look, while others are open to meeting someone but are not looking, instead allowing for real life and serendipitous meetings to occur. There is no right way to go about searching for a partner—in any situation it is important to have a balanced approach that is not based in deep craving.

In either case, in person or online, proximity is required for you to meet the person you are looking for. Whether you are a part of communal spaces where you can meet someone, like work, school, or hobbies, or online spaces where you can come across a potential match, you are putting yourself in situations where you can feel a spark with someone. Once the spark is initiated it becomes possible to have a connection or even a relationship. But no spark can happen without proximity. You cannot have a relationship with someone you do not know. Putting yourself out there by meeting new people will give your intuition opportunities to finally say, "Yes, this is someone you should get to know."

Once you bring yourself into spaces where you can meet someone, the next most important thing is embodiment. The qualities you wish to attract should be the same qualities you are actively developing in yourself. What you are working on will be evident in the way you speak and the way you hold yourself among others. What you embody is an energy you give off combined with the set of actions that you most often repeat. If you are looking for someone who is a good listener, practice listening. If you want to be with someone who can see more perspectives than just their own, you should challenge yourself to see things from multiple angles. If you want someone who cares for their mental health, you should be diligent about finding and using the tools that help your mental health prosper. Whatever it is you are currently working on does not mean that you will necessarily attract someone working on the same exact quality, but it will put out an energy that says, "I am a being who cares about doing the work."

The embodiment of important qualities is a powerful signal that the people around you will respond to. It will bring certain people closer, and it will push others away. Embodiment is not just about having interests or a style of living, it is the active construction of who you are through the intentional application of actions. Embodiment is the result of you being the active designer of your mind and life.

Developing the qualities that you desire in a partner will help you hold yourself well as you move through life. These fundamental qualities that lead to inner and outer harmony are aspects of character that you can use in all situations.

When you are looking for a partner, you are not necessarily hoping for a duplicate of yourself. But you do want someone who can speak the same emotional language. This is why embodiment is important; it will send out the right signal and attract people who are also developing emotional intelligence and maturity.

Again, physical attraction is not enough—that is only what is on the surface. What makes a connection, and ultimately a relationship, happen are the qualities that interlock in supportive ways.

A GROWTH MINDSET IS ESSENTIAL

There is a balance you must walk where you have good standards but at the same time you intentionally strive to not fall into the trap of seeking perfection. This attachment to perfection is insidious; we would all rather have lives where things are smooth and easy and nothing bad ever happens, but that is totally unrealistic. Life is hard, and if we want to get better at dealing with its inevitable highs and lows, our only option is to embrace growth the same way we embrace change, deeply and thoroughly.

When we find our minds clinging to the idea of a perfect partner, we have to mindfully pull ourselves out of that line of thinking because seeking perfection can make us not give our time and energy to someone who could potentially be great for us. It would also be hypocritical since none of us enter relationships as perfect beings ourselves.

Since perfection is never an option, what you can look for is a healthy commitment to growth and evolution. Someone who loves to learn and is not afraid of their emotions will be more inclined to notice what behavior traits are supporting them in living a good life and they will also be honest about what qualities they need to develop that can help them better show up for themselves and other people.

It may sound simple, but being comfortable with the fact that you have room for growth means that you have substantial courage and your ego is not dominating your thought processes. Growth automatically requires humility and the energy of self-love to act on what you know is best for you.

Some of the most beautiful people
are those who have a good balance
between self-love and selflessness.

They take good care of themselves,
work on their growth, and set proper boundaries.
They also treat others well and help when they can.

They know how to be kind
without exhausting themselves.

A BEST FRIEND YOU ARE ATTRACTED TO

One of the most important things you want to look for is someone who just feels like a best friend. So much of a relationship is simply about spending time together. Long-term relationships especially are not about constant highs. In between all the great and memorable moments are the small quiet moments you share together. The ones that some may consider boring and unexciting are actually some of the sweetest moments in a relationship because they are the times when you both feel great just sitting quietly next to each other, where the warmth of your partner's presence is enough. There is joy and harmony in these forgettable moments that should not be overlooked. The fact that you don't have to constantly chase excitement together means you are comfortable with yourselves and your union fulfills you deeply.

Friendship is the part of romantic relationships that is often overlooked. You and your partner should be able to design a space that fully invites vulnerability, one where you are not afraid to give your unfiltered thoughts and you can be your most relaxed selves with each other. A best friend is someone who can appreciate the vast range of your personality. Your partner who loves you should not only be able to embrace the fullness of your range with deep appreciation, but they should also feel a genuine curiosity to know more about each facet of your being as you two spend time together.

The friendship that comes with love should feel like a sigh of relief, where you can finally let your guard down and discuss any topic without the fear of being judged. Making your relationship a space that does not induce fear will end up producing conversations that feed your sense of wonder and discovery.

Sharing quiet space with someone is a rather intimate experience, and it is easier when you feel safe and seen by them. This is why it is especially helpful to have a best friend dynamic with the person you are building a relationship with. Not only do you love them, but you can laugh and process things with them. Falling in love with someone who you also see as a best friend can give you a more expansive relationship. You can care for each other and enjoy life together; you can be deeply honest with each other and laugh together until your eyes are full of joyful tears.

This makes sense when you realize how much time you will spend together, especially if you end up living together and are with each other for years. You would rather do all of this with someone who gets you at every level.

BENEATH THE SURFACE

When you are open to finding a partner, people will come and go as you wait to feel a genuine spark. Once the spark is felt and you both feel the pull of a connection, it does not mean that the discovery process is over. If you understand that a relationship needs more than a connection, you will take the time to get to know an individual so you can really see who they are.

When people initially describe themselves to someone new, they may describe the ideal version of themselves. This is why it is important to see if the way they describe themselves with their words matches up with their actions.

To build a beautiful relationship with someone, you need to know who they are beneath the surface. It is easy to be the best version of yourself when life is running smoothly, but it is a much harder task to meet reality with your best foot forward when things get tough. You do not fully know someone until you see how they deal with challenges.

Are they overwhelmed by their stress? Do they make good decisions when things are chaotic around them? Do they run from their emotions or do they have the strength to face them? If you two have an argument, do they seek to win or are they interested in understanding your perspective and open to sharing theirs?

When you see your new connection deal with something difficult and you get a sense of how deep or intense their reaction is, you can ask yourself, "Is this within a healthy range?"

This is not meant to support the idea that you should hold your partner to an unrealistic standard. Seeking flawless emotional maturity will make you rule out wonderful people. Instead, you are looking for someone who is not afraid to take a good look at themselves, someone who can be mindful of their words, and who is not unconsciously reactive.

If they can stop to think before reacting, this is a big sign that they have grown a lot and are open to more inner development.

The most foundational quality to look for is the simple willingness to grow; this means they have enough humility to expand their perspective and evolve their actions. No matter where they are on their path, they are ready to take steps forward. The surface of the ocean hides what is underneath. Human beings are just as deep as an ocean. Even if an individual is not intentionally hiding who they are, it will be quite difficult to really know them after spending just a few moments together. Only by going through different experiences with them will more of what is underneath be revealed.

Every individual is a mosaic of experiences, conditioning, impulses, strengths, fears, aspirations, and more. As you look for your partner, you need to see if they not only fit well in your arms, but if your two mosaics add to each other's inner beauty and harmony.

If your past partner was emotionally unavailable
and did not take care of your heart,
you will have to be intentional about
putting down your guard when you
meet someone new.

The same defensive pattern that protected you before
can stop a new connection from fully flourishing.

FIVE RED FLAGS AND FIVE GREEN FLAGS

When you see a connection forming, you have to be honest with yourself about whether or not the person you have chemistry with also has the qualities that are needed to help you create a thriving relationship. It is common to feel strongly for someone and not have the skills to elevate that connection into a loving and nourishing partnership. It is not reasonable to expect perfection, but there does need to be the intention to learn from your imperfections.

Connection plus the willingness to grow are the two main qualities that are needed, but from there people are quite varied in what they are looking for. Two individuals who have the energy and self-awareness to elevate their connection into a loving relationship are essentially designing a new culture that is just for them—their own precious world that fits their needs, wants, preferences, and is built on their understanding of each other.

Even though every love is unique, there are still qualities that can block a relationship from forming and ones that set you up for success.

Five Red Flags

1. **Pretending to know everything.** The space of knowledge is limitless. Acting as if we have much to teach and

nothing to learn is a clear sign that ego has overtaken the mind and made it rigid. Being open to learning and saying sentences like, "I don't know much about that; can you tell me more?" demonstrates the type of humility that is based upon inner strength. Without humility, you cannot grow.

2. **It is hard to learn anything about them.** If they just ask you questions and don't want to talk about themselves, there is an unwillingness to be vulnerable there. If they are hiding who they are, how can you connect well? Some people see mystery as an attractive quality, but if taken to an extreme the one you are attracted to will always remain a stranger. Being open is needed for a connection to become something deeper.

3. **Not being honest with themselves**. If they are constantly overestimating their capacity and saying they will do certain things but in the end don't show up, this is a sign that they struggle to face their own truth. Not being honest with yourself and not having the courage to speak that truth is what leads to ghosting. Lying to yourself is also one of the deeper roots of people-pleasing. Being honest about what you can and can't do makes you more dependable and creates the environment of safety and trust that a long-lasting relationship is built on.

4. **No accountability.** If they have a hard time admitting when they are wrong or apologizing when they have made a mistake, it will be hard to create a culture between the two of you where you are actively learning from your mistakes and using them as a gateway for growth. Owning up to a mistake and using the information to change your habits or responses to situations is a great sign of self-awareness and maturity.

5. **Making things good for themselves, but not for you.** If they are deeply focused on their own preferences while the two of you are together and are not interested in doing things that you like, then they are showing signs of being self-centered. A connection should have synergy, a clear back-and-forth that allows both of you to feel heard. One of the fun parts of a relationship is getting to create a new culture together, but if one person is dominating everything, the other will eventually feel like they have no power in the relationship.

Five Green Flags

1. **Listening with calm enjoyment.** It can be felt when they ask you questions not out of a sense of obligation but out of genuine curiosity. If they listen to your answers with focus and are feeling real joy from getting to

know you, this is a sign that they are not self-centered. Listening is the road you need to travel to deepen any connection.

2. **A willingness to be vulnerable**. As you build on a connection, you eventually need to start sharing the harder parts of yourselves and the parts of your emotional histories that only those closest to you know. Vulnerability is how you open your hearts to each other. Your partner can only know and understand you if you have the strength to be vulnerable—they need this information to be able to show up for you well. Love and vulnerability go hand in hand, they elevate each other.

3. **The energy is reciprocal.** There is a feeling of balance when you spend time with them. You are both sharing, listening, taking turns leading, learning from each other, and more. Just as you are willing to let them into your life, they are also making space for you in theirs. You can both feel each other's excitement and you are both revitalized by the other's presence.

4. **They feel joy when they see you happy.** In a lot of long-term relationships, people say that seeing their partner happy is one of their biggest joys. This does not just happen after years of being together, it can also happen in the beginning. Another person's radiance activat-

ing your own radiance is a sign of deep compassion. This means that they can join you in the good moments and that they also have a greater potential to work through the harder moments with you.

5. **They are actively working on developing new qualities.** Having the self-awareness to know that they are imperfect but would benefit greatly from developing new positive habits and behaviors is truly empowering. Asking the question "What are you currently working on internally?" can be very revealing. If they say they are improving their ability to respond instead of reacting, or developing more patience, or trying to see things from more perspectives than just their own, you will have some clear signs that they are committed to deep inner work.

Reflection Questions

- What qualities do you want in a partner?
- What emotional skills do you want your partner to have?
- Is the person you are building with committed to growth and open to communication?
- What are you doing to be a good partner?
- Are you putting yourself out there to be able to find the right person? If not, how could you do this authentically?

chapter 12

The Foundations of a Good Relationship

HONESTY

A relationship that is genuine has honesty at its center. To be able to create a home where both people feel safe, seen, and properly held, there needs to be a foundation of honesty that bridges the communication. Honesty is a fundamental characteristic of a healthy union. When it is present in a relationship it can create a multitude of benefits while its absence will ultimately lead to disarray and hurt.

A partner should be a haven, a being who you feel undeniably comfortable with and someone you know is ready to face the ups and downs of life with you. A partner is not an ordinary connection. The two of you made the special choice to mold your lives together, to start facing the world as a team. Coming together in a relationship as equal partners who both have strengths that each of you can lean on will help you tackle challenges with the best solutions possible, ones that you conjure up together.

To be able to have such a partnership, you have to challenge yourself to step forward with your truth when you are interacting with your partner. If you want a beautiful partnership that is evolving into greater heights of love and care, you need to make sure to do your part and overcome the fear of disappointing the one you love.

It can feel especially difficult to have open discussions if you have experienced a childhood where the truth was not welcomed and instead it was encouraged to simply act like everything was okay for the sake of "keeping the peace." In these situations, the tension that the truth may cause by bringing things out into the open does not go away when you remain silent. Rather, the tension will stay within you because you actively have to suppress the truth instead of dealing with the tension as a group and coming to a solution that will ultimately relieve the heaviness. You either have to allow the tension to arise, speak the truth, and lay it out so that things can be dealt with, or you will have to carry the burden of the truth that remains unspoken. Even small lies can weigh heavily on your mind.

You have to remind yourself that an emotionally mature relationship is not possible when you are feeding each other lies. Even if lies were silently supported while you were growing up, you need to break this cycle and stop repeating this pattern if you want your relationship to thrive. As most people would rather hear the truth than a lie, we should respect our partners enough to give them exactly what we ask for, despite the initial discomfort. Our own temporary discomfort is not a good enough reason to withhold the truth from the person we love so deeply. We may say we are just doing it out of ease, that it doesn't really matter, but it does matter a great deal when you are placing your own comfort above the trust your partner has in you to be open and honest with them.

The truth can sometimes hurt at first because a wound or mistake is being revealed. In the act of revealing the wound, there are two potential paths: Either the wound becomes worse, or it is given the opportunity to heal. It takes a lot of strength to come forward with the truth because it can feel risky—especially if the truth is a big one. But ultimately, revealing the truth gives you the opportunity to connect more deeply and vulnerably and to live more peacefully after everything is settled, as opposed to living with the tension of a lie.

The advantage of living with the truth is that you can enhance your partnership deeply. Lies create distance between you and yourself and you and your partner. Being honest in your relationship helps you double down on openness and it deepens your understanding of each other. To make your union stronger, you need to give each other your vulnerability. Being able to see each other's mistakes and raw emotions allows you to process your lives together at a deeper level. The basic truth is that you two cannot fully understand each other if you are not being honest with each other. Communication is not happening if the truth is missing; if one person is lying, that is called deception.

Without honesty there cannot be trust and without trust the feeling of safety that you give each other will melt away. Lies stop your relationship from evolving. They are also a sign that you don't fully trust your partner and that you perceive them as unaccepting.

Three things make a relationship exceptional:

When you are both good at letting go
of petty arguments.

When neither of you seeks perfection but
you each agree to put in clear effort.

When you find joy in meeting each other's needs.

INDIVIDUALIZED CARE

Love is a powerful feeling and state of mind, but it does not inherently guarantee that the two people love connects will have a harmonious relationship. It is quite common to love someone without knowing how to properly care for them. It is painful to be the one giving amply to the relationship and, even though you know your partner loves you, see them struggle to care for you properly. It is also painful to feel the depth of a connection and see that you are struggling to give the connection what it needs to flourish.

Before you can remedy this struggle, you need to embrace the realization that you can feel strongly for someone and there may still be a gap between the two of you, a gap that can only be filled with the intentional learning of how to care for each other.

Love is an invitation to grow. When you start noticing that you need to strengthen certain qualities to improve the way you care for your partner (qualities like selfless listening, honesty, entering conversations with vulnerability, trust, patience, seeing outside of your own perspective, etc.) your love for them should help support your humility to accept and act on your need to grow. Love should energize you into embracing your evolution so that you can cultivate good qualities that truly benefit your relationship and any interactions that you may have as you move through life.

People who have healed deeply
and know their worth cannot
help but emit "love me well
or leave me alone" energy.

They only allow real connections
with people who are emotionally
ready because they know
relationships take a certain
degree of work.

Care is not intuitive for everyone, especially because individuals are strikingly unique. The way people like to be cared for varies massively. Each individual will feel cared for by very different sets of actions. Some may be able to smoothly ease into caring for their partner, while others may find caring for their partner more doable after many conversations where both partners make their needs and wants clear. In any case, there will be a need for learning. Time and space dedicated to simply understanding your partner's preferences are necessary in any relationship. Likewise, we cannot force our partner to act just as we wish them to, but we can try to discuss and make voluntary commitments in how we treat the other to best meet each other's needs.

Many have this notion that the right partner will come fully equipped with all the emotional development necessary to make the relationship successful, but this is far from the truth. Only after two people are able to see and know each other well does it become possible for harmony to flow. Deep care is possible after you spend time understanding each other's emotional histories, your strengths and fears, and how you've dealt with challenges you have each faced in the past. We often fall into the misconception of thinking our partner will want to receive love the way we prefer to receive it, but this is not true, and it takes open communication and switching your perspective to fix this error.

Love is the home you share and care is the way you design the inside of your home so that it feels vibrant, safe, and rejuvenating. Let love bring you together, but do not expect the feelings you have for each other to fix every issue that comes up. Show your partner you love them by caring for them well.

Let your partner know what
they are doing right.

Don't let the things that support
your happiness be a mystery to them.

Clarity and positive feedback are needed
if you are seeking to build a home
that is nourishing for the both of you.

FUN

There is a special type of joy that only the two of you can give each other. Not only do you each feel right in the other's arms, but your union is the creation of a new world, one that is just for the two of you. You create your own culture together, you share inside jokes, you have overlapping preferences, you even sometimes go as far as developing your own quirky language together. In the safety of each other's nonjudgmental presence, you both relax enough to find the joy that is missing from your regular daily life. Of course you do all the mundane and repetitive things together too, but they aren't as tedious when you have someone you love to share them with.

Not only are you deeply attracted to your partner, but they are also your best friend, and they have a sense of humor that you greatly enjoy.

In a world that moves at such an incredible speed, one that is hyper focused on productivity, you and your partner create a small island of togetherness where fun and deep connection can very easily arise. These small moments may end up being some of your most cherished.

Eleven Attributes of a Thriving Relationship

1. **You work as a team.** You both know that you have different strengths and you let them shine as you take on challenges together. Depending on the situation, you let the partner with that strength take the lead because what you want most is a process and an outcome that the both of you feel good about.

2. **You understand that not every day will be a great day.** Part of love is letting go of perfection; you know that it is natural to have ups and downs and that joy is not an ever-flowing constant. You use the down moments as opportunities to support each other.

3. **You both embrace growth.** Love is the clearest mirror that will reveal your strengths and the qualities you need to keep cultivating. You don't fear your own imperfection, instead you embrace the challenge to take your evolution into your own hands. You know that the more you grow, not only will your personal happiness expand but you will also be able to love your partner better.

4. **You understand that the deepest happiness comes from within.** You both have enough wisdom to not give the responsibility of your happiness to another person.

You know your partner can certainly add to the beauty of life but that ultimately your personal perceptions and reactions are the biggest factors that impact your happiness. You know that your happiness is a puzzle that only you can solve.

5. **You are both intentional about being present with each other.** Life can get really busy, but you make sure to create space for the two of you to reconnect and share honestly and openly about how you have been. You always make it a point to keep developing your connection.

6. **Conflict is an opportunity to understand each other.** Disagreements are natural but you do your best to not make it about winning, instead you try to understand each other's perspective. You practice selfless listening so you can really take in how the series of events occurred in your partner's mind.

7. **Vulnerability and honesty are welcome.** You understand that lies create distance that can limit the strength of your connection. One of the ways you love each other well is by letting your truth come forward and by putting your guard down so you can deeply know one another.

8. **Laughter and rest are a central part of your union.** Your connection is vibrant, and you enjoy each other's company so deeply that it is easy to make each other laugh. You are good at slowing down together when needed by letting the other know what your energy levels are. The same way you take on the world together, you also close the doors to it so you can fully recharge.

9. **You let each other change.** The reality is that who you both were when you fell in love and who you are now is quite different. You accept the fact that your likes and dislikes will evolve over time. You use this truth as a way to remain curious about each other.

10. **You don't control each other.** You know that freedom is the centerpiece of love, and that control creates friction that can fracture a beautiful connection. Instead, you talk to each other about what you can voluntarily commit to. This will make how you function as a unit clear to the both of you.

11. **You don't take each other for granted**. As time moves forward, you don't let the busyness of life allow you to forget to appreciate your partner. Within your mind and in your actions, you intentionally rekindle the feeling of gratitude that you have for each other.

THE PARADOX OF GROWTH

Love cannot flourish at its highest level if your partner does not love you as you are now, beauty and flaws together. Imperfection is genuinely what makes you special—your partner should love you completely without the desire to change you. If they are constantly nagging you about changing different aspects of yourself, then what they desire is an image of you they have in their mind as opposed to the real you that is right in front of them.

This type of change is different from how we are constantly-changing beings, as it takes intention and application to evolve in a certain direction. When left to nature, everything grows and decays, but if you want to grow in a particular way it takes intentional action and effort applied over time.

Since we are deeply patterned beings, it is difficult to change quickly, even when you and your partner see a change that needs to be made. Transformation begins with intention and is then made possible through repeated attempts. Even if you want to change overnight, it will be hard to overcome years of dense patterning that is pushing your behaviors in a particular direction. Granted, determination makes a big difference and can help you effect changes quickly, but that is not always the case for everyone. Normally, change is gradual and it takes time and consistent effort for the new you to fully arise. Patience with yourself and from your partner are vital when you are working on growing; this will give you the grace needed when you make mistakes along the way and the strength needed to continue on.

The tricky thing about relationships is that they often glaringly point a mirror at what you need to work on. What is important to understand is that the desire to grow has to come from within you, it cannot come from your partner demanding it of you. The energy to change has to come from your own volition for it to be potent and long-lasting. If you try to change solely because your partner wants you to change, this will eventually lead to resentment and it can be quite damaging to your sense of self-worth. Being with someone who does not see you as enough is painful and not an unconditional form of love. On the other hand, clearly seeing your flaws and recognizing that both you and your partner would benefit from you putting energy into changing them is the right mindset for building a new way of being. But this should be a two-way street. Each partner should be able to discuss ways they'd like to see their partner grow in a calm and mindful manner. If your partner is always nagging you about changing multiple aspects of your character, they may be coming to you from a place of craving, especially since they are clearly struggling to love you as you are.

The relationship will make it obvious how you need to grow and sometimes your partner may tell you that directly, which isn't always a bad thing. Sometimes they will be able to see one of your blocks much more clearly than you can. Especially if your partner is coming from a loving place, it is a service to you to tell you about a characteristic that is making things relationally or professionally difficult for you. They are telling you not because they will love you more if you change, but because they think life will be smoother for you if you adjust your actions. It can feel quite challenging to hear the truth from them, but it may also be the wake-up call we need, especially if we have the humility to receive it well.

The paradox of growth in a relationship is that your partner should love you as you are, and that love should inspire you to grow. For many, love creates such a deep sense of safety that we feel energized to take on healing ourselves and growing in ways that we have not before. Often we put so much energy into simply getting through life that it is a shock to have a genuinely loving and supportive relationship. Within this supportive space you find you now have energy to focus on deeper matters of the mind and heart that need resolving. Even though your partner loves you as you are, being in their presence can give you a new sense of determination to evolve into the best you possible. A supportive and loving partnership can give you the ability to restructure life so you have a clear sense of your priorities. A lot of the energy that you used to put into finding a partner can be redirected to enjoying and growing with the partner you now have.

Being in a relationship is of course not necessary to grow deeply, but for many it becomes a catalyst for reaching new levels of self-understanding and compassion for yourself and the people who cross your path. A relationship is like a training ground for the development of qualities that are valuable in all parts of your life. Being able to see perspectives outside of your own, having patience, managing your reactions so they don't get overblown—these are all qualities we can improve while in a relationship and we can make use of them in our work and life.

Relationships are not about trying to change each other, but if the love is real and all-encompassing, this generative energy can function like fertile soil that can support you to blossom in new and unforeseen ways. Great relationships can encourage you to grow and evolve to the point where you shine in previously unseen ways.

Reflection Questions

- What are the strengths that you bring to your relationship? What are your partner's strengths? How do you care for each other?
- How are you doing with being honest in your relationship? Could you be more forthright and open?
- Are there any truths you are holding on to out of fear that are keeping you from connecting more deeply with your partner?
- What are some voluntary commitments you and your partner have made with each other? Are there any new ones you want to discuss with them?
- What are some ways you and your partner could introduce more fun into your relationship?
- How are you supporting your own happiness?

chapter 13

Love Is Freedom

What does it mean to feel free in a relationship?

Love and freedom go hand in hand, especially when they arise within the individual. The wisest people on earth, those who cross the threshold of enlightenment, develop minds that can only see through the eyes of love. Malice is eradicated from the heart, the will to harm is erased, the urge to create disharmony is burned away, the ego is no more. The only things that flourish in the mind of someone who is fully free are the stunning clarity of love and compassion and a deep understanding of reality and nature.

For freedom to be fully accessed, the mind needs to utterly embrace the universal law of impermanence, the truth that everything is always changing. It seems straightforward at the intellectual level, but this truth is one that we always fight because the mind is inclined toward attachment. To study this truth, to feel this truth so deeply that the mind never again doubts or forgets that the ever-changing flow of nature is happening around us and within us—this opens the door to freedom. The goal of freedom requires you to walk a path that deeply embraces change; this path dissolves the ego and when you arrive at your destination the mind and heart become completely and utterly loving.

Taking the human mind to the pinnacle of evolution by turning the attention inward and cultivating deep self-awareness is in itself an act of love. The beauty of taking this path is that every step results in increased growth and compassion. You don't have to achieve the ultimate goal before you see real and transformative results that positively impact every relationship and aspect of your life. The two qualities of love and freedom support each other: Cultivating freedom enhances your ability to love, cultivating love makes you more and more free. To develop either requires the dissolution of ego and the repeated act of letting go so you are no longer attached to anything. The deep embrace of change makes the evaporation of ego and attachment much more efficient. Choosing freedom instead of suffering results in a being of boundless love.

When the mind is no longer driven by ego, it starts to sit comfortably in compassion. It is possible for a mind that used to only see itself and its cravings to unfold and release these attachments so it can start comprehending that its well-being is as important as the well-being of others. The mind is incredibly elastic and malleable; it does not need to remain in its basic survivalist format, which tends to look at the world through fearful eyes. Compassion has the uncanny ability to preserve the safety of a human being while also creating openings for genuine thriving. Compassion is real intelligence because it helps you see the wide range of human experience, while fear keeps you self-centered. Compassion helps you act skillfully and helps you find new solutions for old problems.

The struggle of the human being is that dissatisfaction or suffering is a consistent part of human life. This is one of the main reasons that people turn inward, to find the roots of human suffering and hopefully a path out of that suffering. There are many traditions around the world that have ways of cultivating the human mind, in fact most cultures have methods to elevate the human mind in some manner or another, but what is consistently clear is that when someone finds and applies useful methods to undo the tension of the mind, their practice will result in a more loving mind: love for themselves and love for all beings. The mind feels a tremendous ease when it grows its ability to love, mainly because true love is a state of detachment, unconditioned. You learn to observe as opposed to crave, you help without the need to control or receive recognition, you apply effort without being attached to the results, you have goals and act toward them without having your happiness dependent on them, you love unconditionally.

There are beings alive now and in the past who have truly taken the mind to its apex. The full flowering of the human mind results in boundless unconditional love; it creates a mind that no longer sees anyone as an enemy. It is a mind without tension, having only clarity and precision, and it can only produce acts that have the intention of compassion. In a way it can be said that the arc of human evolution bends toward love. Love is the home we desire because we have felt its powerful impact and see its potential inside every single one of us. Granted, to become a fully enlightened human who loves all beings unconditionallly is exceedingly rare. But we all have that seed of freedom inside of us.

The apex of unconditional love may seem far away, but you get a taste of it in your everyday life.

You can see that drive to love and how powerful it is by looking at the microcosm of relationships. You can get a glimpse into the possibility of loving someone without attachments when you do your best to love your partner better. A relationship becomes this great opportunity to practice supporting each other's freedom. Your partnership is an opportunity to practice building a balance between having your needs met and making sure that you are also attentive to their needs. A healthy relationship asks the both of you to not be selfish. This applies to all loving relationships in our lives, friends, family, children. We give and receive love in all these instances and balance it with our self-love and care.

True love will require you to create an environment that

is not one of control, domination, or self-centeredness, but one that is instead based on balance, harmony, and mutual trust and respect. A relationship is the space where we practice love and learn how to expand our horizon of what love encompasses. For the love between the two of you to last, you will have to welcome forgiveness, which is essentially letting go, since mistakes will be made. The same qualities you develop to maintain a healthy relationship overlap greatly with the qualities needed to be an enlightened human being.

Since relationships are centered around love and, in their most evolved form, love's elevation into the feeling of freedom, it would be worthwhile to clearly delineate what it means to feel free in a relationship. The mind may reactively jump into thinking about freedom as a sense of lawlessness where each partner can do whatever they want without worry, but that is not real freedom, that is simply selfishness and craving without end. The freedom that is supported by the love of a relationship is centered on the radical and rare ability to be your truest self. This doesn't just mean feeling safe to be vulnerable and feeling like you can say the unfiltered thoughts of your mind, but it also means being the rawest version of yourself. *To show your partner the sides of you that are deeply afraid, wounded, misunderstood; to show the one you love the full spectrum of your personality is in itself an act of freedom.* To be able to feel so open with another person is only possible if the love between you is strong, active, and unquestionable.

Five Ways to Support the Feeling of Freedom in Your Relationship

1. **Give selflessly.** To feel free in a relationship not only means that you do your best to care for each other well and support your partner's happiness, but you also make it your mission to understand each other. This is where a lot of relationships tend to fail; care and support fall flat if you give care and support the way you desire it, as opposed to the way your partner needs it.

   You and your partner are very different people and this makes your individual preferences unique. You can feel like you are giving so much to them, but you are actually not offering them the thing that they want, in the way they can best receive it. Because understanding is missing, the two of you end up feeling far away from each other. Understanding can never be overlooked when you are committed to doing your part to make the love you share vibrant. When you really understand your partner's preferences and are trying to meet their desires, your giving will be much more effective.

2. **Love with the least attachment possible.** The healthiest relationships do not rely on attachment, instead they are built on communication and intentional commitments. Before you can even get to a space of designing

your relationship intentionally in a way that feels good to the both of you, you have to do a lot of self-examination and see how many of your actions are being driven by your attachments. Attachments can squeeze the air out of a relationship, because they are the opposite of freedom. The attachments that exist in your mind manifest as control in the physical world.

3. **Practice preventive communication.** Understanding how your partner is feeling and thinking will help you know how to support them. These preferences may change over time, just like everything in the universe, so it is helpful to check in repeatedly. Communication is especially important when you want to understand where your partner is in their emotional spectrum. Share the changes in your feelings before they snowball into something bigger. The mind will try to trick itself into a fight. Speaking up and letting each other know when you are feeling down or when your mood is heavy can be really helpful with stopping unnecessary arguments from happening.

   Preventive communication gives you the information you need to really be compassionate with each other. If you know your partner is going through a tough moment, it will inspire you to care for them in a way that helps relieve things. It will help you have compassion for them. Even though the heavy mood is happening within them, the love and care you give them can certainly make things easier as their inner storm passes through.

It is also important to let each other know when you feel great. This way you can both know when to be more playful and adventurous. Being aware of each other's upshifts and downshifts gives you the information you need to adapt and reshape what supporting the other's happiness looks like.

4. **Build your home around commitments.** Love is the opposite of coercion. Love does not seek to control. Love does not have any ill will. Love functions best through the mediums of compassion and understanding. To really love each other better, challenge yourselves to not demand things from each other. Instead let your needs and wants become clearly known and then allow your partner the opportunity to see what they can voluntarily commit to. Like this, the two of you can take turns and make up-front commitments with each other about how your relationship will function.

   These voluntary commitments are essentially the culture of your relationship. You are designing your environment together in such a way that you both feel empowered and well-informed. There are no secrets regarding what you genuinely want from your relationship.

You don't ever expect your partner to read your mind. Being vocal with each other about how you each plan on showing up for the relationship will support the feeling of safety that the two of you are mutually creating.

You are committed to each other out of sheer love, not out of control or fear. The willingness to show up for your partner comes directly from your own heart, which makes the magical aspects of a relationship much more possible. Energy that is freely given is far more powerful than energy that is taken.

5. **Meet your partner again and again.** Throughout the length of your relationship, you and your partner will continue flowing along the forward river of time, which means who you were when you first met will be long gone and what you will actually have of each other is the person right in front of you. Who you once were together is a memory that can give you a sense of who your partner is, but it cannot paint the entirety of the picture. To really see your partner, you will have to observe them in the present moment. Getting to know who your partner is now requires more than the regular day-to-day communication; it takes going deeper.

Goal:

Only do what feels genuinely right
and let everything else go.

THE HEALING GENERATION IS LEARNING HOW TO LOVE BETTER

We live in a special time in human history when millions around the world are actively healing themselves of past trauma, old hurt, and the tension that makes the mind heavy. In a big way, being miserable is going out of style. Fewer people are resorting to running away from their suffering or spending their lives suppressing it. It has become more common than ever to see a therapist, to have a meditation practice, to be open about mental health struggles and victories, and it feels like society at large is embracing that life is about much more than productivity. The inner world of the mind and heart is becoming as important as the outer life of work and community. In fact, we are collectively learning that the inner and the outer are deeply intertwined, that they push and pull on each other, and the heaviness of one can negatively impact the other.

You can feel it when a person has overcome
serious challenges in life and has transformed
into a better version of themselves.

Their vibe is striking and
their confidence has a special glow.

A healing generation has emerged that is serious about overcoming internal burdens and making the access to healing tools more widely available to people across the world. The healing of the heart and mind is a profoundly personal and intimate experience, a journey that can transform an individual's life—but what we are starting to see now is that this deeply personal journey is causing waves that are directing humanity to understand what a healthy relationship looks like.

From generation to generation, sorrow was passed down as a regular part of culture, until the healing generation that we are currently in emerged. Those of us alive today collectively said, "That is enough."

This historical moment of self-observation, which was fueled by the self-love and mental health movement, is not only showing us that individuals need to heal, but it is also showing us that we need to collectively learn how to love one another better so that healthy relationships can become more common. We are not only acting on the dire need for individuals to find and use methods that can alleviate the mind and clarify our perceptions, but we are also seeing that the inner work has an immediate impact on our relationships.

As we started developing compassion, patience, and kindness toward ourselves, we realized that we did not need to keep these qualities to ourselves; we could share them with those who were in our immediate proximity. Especially with the ones we love the most. The healing of the individual showed us that our relationships needed healing too, that we could figure out better ways to show up in our relationships, to care for each other, to move beyond connection and into active love. In a very direct way, the healing of the individual sparked a renewed interest in figuring out how to have healthy and vibrant relationships.

The connection between the two makes sense because we can only give what is within us, and as our inner capacity expands, we are able to give and receive more in our partnerships. The healing generation has started a massive shift in global culture that will continue reverberating through the decades and generations to come. Not only is misery going out of style, but so is having low-quality relationships. The same way we instinctively knew that it was possible to have a better and deeper relationship with ourselves, we also know it is possible to experience the love of a relationship in a much more generative way.

It still feels like we are at the beginning, but enough is different now that there is no going back. We have pressed upon history and shifted its direction. We have collectively made individual healing important; we have also brought great attention to the need for healthier and more fulfilling relationships. People who are healing are increasing their ability to love, not just their partners but their children, family, and friends as well. All the inner and relational work that is happening is creating a less traumatized humanity, one that can love further, love selflessly, and love actively.

Emotional maturity does not create
a perfect relationship, it just sets you up
to better handle the ups and downs
that are bound to happen while you
learn to love each other well.

Long conversations, tears, apologies,
and embracing vulnerability are
common when the love is deep.

Learning how to love better is a lifelong journey. My advice to you is don't be hard on yourself for how you were in the past; use it as motivation to act differently in the present and future. None of us are perfect and even when you have the best of intentions, someone may still misunderstand you, but one of the most fortunate aspects of life is that we have the opportunity to try again with those still around us. Whether it is the love in your own heart or the love you give to those who are dearest to you, you have the chance to expand what that love looks like and how much it encompasses.

As I stated in the first chapter, there are three qualities that will make the biggest difference in your ability to love better: kindness, growth, and compassion. You can simplify everything by just focusing on these three qualities and measuring if they are maturing within you.

If you stay committed to kindness, that which you give to yourself and to your partner, it will help smooth out the little moments of turmoil and misunderstanding so that they don't become major blocks or points of pain in your history together. Treating each other with kindness does not mean being fake, it means slowing down and taking a moment to recognize that this person in front of you is incredibly important. They are the person you are building your home with, the one who is your comrade in life. Remember, they are one of the most precious sights your eyes have ever encountered. Taking the time to remind yourself that the person you share your life with is a magical human being is how you activate loving-kindness, and it inspires you to treat them with gentleness. Giving your undivided presence to the one you love is an act of kindness that fuels your connection—it keeps the bond between the two of you strong, it helps your love feel alive.

Maintaining a serious and lifelong commitment to growth is one of the most challenging things we can do. This requires you to keep the value of humility high on your list of what's important. Without humility, the ego will get bigger, and it will eventually dissuade you from finding growth necessary. The ego loves to be stagnant, it does not like change, and it certainly does not want any challenges to the sense of self it is attached to. Humility helps the ego not become an overconsuming aspect of your mind. Humility is what helps you see beyond your own perspective, and it helps you see that you are not always right. Having the humility to admit there is room for improvement and to act on that with self-development is one of the most beautiful aspects of character that a human being can have. It takes a lot of strength to remain malleable and adaptive. Especially when fear and old hurt want you to become hard and rigid, you intentionally choose softness because only through the strength of softness can you change your form. Seeing the ways you can grow and acting on them is necessary when you want to share quality years and decades with the one you love. As time moves forward and life changes, the two of you will also change in ways that help the light of love stay lit.

Compassion is the quality that makes hard times softer. There are going to be countless ups and downs, even in the healthiest and most loving relationships. The way you two interact will not be perfect and there will be moments when you do not align well, but even in the midst of disharmony you will be able to find your way back to balance by choosing compassion as your medium of interaction. You need humility to see beyond your own perspective, but you also need compassion to be able to fully understand and relate to what your partner is going through. Compassion is an act of selflessness that helps the two of you come closer together. Compassion is actually a practice in letting go; you are momentarily forgoing your view of how things happen in order to step into your partner's shoes and see things from their viewpoint. Having this wider sense of perspective can help you forgive more easily, and it can help you understand where tough emotions are coming from. Compassion does not mean you become a people pleaser or that you allow your partner to step all over you. Compassion has to work both ways—you need to have it for yourself and for your partner.

Each quality requires balance. If you take any of these to an extreme, it will throw off your inner harmony and the harmony of the relationship. You have to know when to apply each quality and how much. Too much kindness can become disingenuous and make you bypass big issues that you truly need to talk about. Focusing too much on growth can make you forget you are whole and amazing just as you are and it does not give you time to integrate steps forward. Too much compassion toward yourself can make you selfish, and too much for your partner can make you set aside your personal needs and wants in a relationship and lead to burnout.

The main thing all relationships need is balance. Both people have to feel like they are giving and receiving. If one person is doing all the emotional heavy lifting, all the forgiving, all the problem-solving and leading, then things will start to turn sideways for the relationship. You both should feel like equals in the relationship. Even though you both have different strengths and preferences, you should both feel that your power is helping design the culture of what love looks like in your home. You are both leaders in your relationship, even if that leadership looks different for each of you.

If you are ever in doubt about how to love your partner better, just ask. Do not measure yourself by the other couples you know. The way your love is shaped is unique and that's what makes it so special. You have to make the way you love your own, because you and your partner cannot be duplicated.

The people I admire the most
are the ones who unabashedly
tend to their inner peace.

They do not want to hurt anyone.
They move with kindness.
They make time for self-care and growth.
They do their best to give compassion
to all those who cross their path.
These people make the world lighter.

ON LOVE AND THE WORLD

Living from a place of love is an extraordinary challenge. Treating yourself well, staying in tune with your intuition, understanding and unpacking your emotional history, all this is a large task on its own. It takes work to keep love flowing within you but living from love asks even more of you.

Love is an elevating force that cannot just stay within you—it seeks to shine outward and brighten the world. If happiness and inner peace are what you seek, then love is the only path forward.

First you have to develop it within yourself so it can blossom in all the unknown and unhealed parts of your being. If your self-love is true and deep it will keep increasing and make your love for family and friends much clearer and more selfless. Genuine self-love will eventually create the beginnings of unconditional love for all beings. When you really start understanding yourself and the emotions you move through, you begin to see that all human beings are going through the same spectrum of emotions and experiences. Even though each person has their own unique experience of life, we are all feeling the same set of emotions, just at different frequencies and intensities. Understanding this will show you how similar we all are and help expand your compassion for all beings.

Love is not just a form of care, it also carries essential wisdom, it teaches the liberating lesson that if you seek to be truly free you have to enhance your perspective so that more beings are encompassed by your compassion. Having love for all beings does not mean you have to be friends or agree with everyone, especially when others are causing harm. It simply means you are no longer interested in directly or indirectly harming others. It means you want others to be happy, to be loved, to be peaceful, to be healed, to have the resources they need to thrive.

By far the most difficult part of love is when you or someone close to you is harmed. The immediate reaction is often to return that harm to another, to make them feel what you felt. But retribution rarely creates external safety, and it can never create internal peace—it just widens the circle of harm and creates more people who need healing. With enough wisdom it becomes clear that intentionally harming another wreaks havoc on your mind and fills your subconscious with great tension that will sit with you today and impact your tomorrow. Harm that comes to a loved one can also stem from illness or accidents, with no one we can directly blame. It can be very difficult to watch a loved one go through this incredibly difficult experience and not be able to help or save them. Much of life is outside of our control and sometimes the most we can do is be there for our loved ones and give our presence and support.

Love sees no one as an enemy, but this does not mean it resigns you to a passive existence. Love can protect and preserve itself and those being harmed when it needs to, using strength and power, not with the intention to harm others, but to stop harm. Love can inspire your actions and make them skillful, as opposed to reactive. By its very nature love cannot act from a place of hate. Where hate seeks to dominate, control, and even destroy, love will do its best to produce generative actions that expand the bounty of joy and freedom. Love calls us to move in the direction of egolessness, to let go of fear and hierarchy and to treat each other with genuine kindness. The love within you will be in direct alignment with how you express love in the world.

Love is the condition needed for true harmony to exist. Love is a tiny revolution that happens in the human heart, that ultimately produces large waves of change. Love is a supremely clear perspective that helps you see the falsehood of all divisions. Let love become the lens you use to see yourself and the world. Let love inspire your actions and your life.

You have no idea how much
impact your kindness has.

Without even knowing,
you have turned bad days into great ones,
you have reconnected people with their power,
and you have helped many realize
that there is still some good in the world.

Having someone love you
exactly as you are is a liberating gift.

You feel at home because you
know you are safe in their presence.

Their acceptance of you unlocks a
deep sense of rest that revitalizes your being.

It's not about looking for a perfect partner;
it's about looking for someone who is ready for love.

Ready doesn't mean you have it all figured out;
it just means you are aware of your imperfections
and want to put energy into your growth.

Find someone who can blossom with you.

Reflection Questions

- Are you putting time and energy into growing your capacity for unconditional love?
- What are new ways you want to expand your selfless love?
- How does your partner prefer to receive love? Could you be doing more to love them how they want to be loved?
- Do you feel free in your relationship? In what ways could you feel freer and how can you work toward this?
- How are you developing your kindness, growth, and compassion within your relationships? What are some small ways you can bring these more into your consistent actions?

ABOUT THE AUTHOR

Yung Pueblo is the pen name of the writer Diego Perez and means "young people." The name is meant to convey that humanity is entering an era of remarkable growth and healing, when many will expand their self-awareness and release old burdens. He is the #1 *New York Times* bestselling author of *Lighter* and the Inward Trilogy. He lives in western Massachusetts with his wife, Sara.

yungpueblo.com

ABOUT THE TYPE

This book was set in Baskerville, a typeface designed by John Baskerville (1706–75), an amateur printer and typefounder, and cut for him by John Handy in 1750. The type became popular again when the Lanston Monotype Corporation of London revived the classic roman face in 1923. The Mergenthaler Linotype Company in England and the United States cut a version of Baskerville in 1931, making it one of the most widely used typefaces today.